CHILDREN AS FILM MAKERS

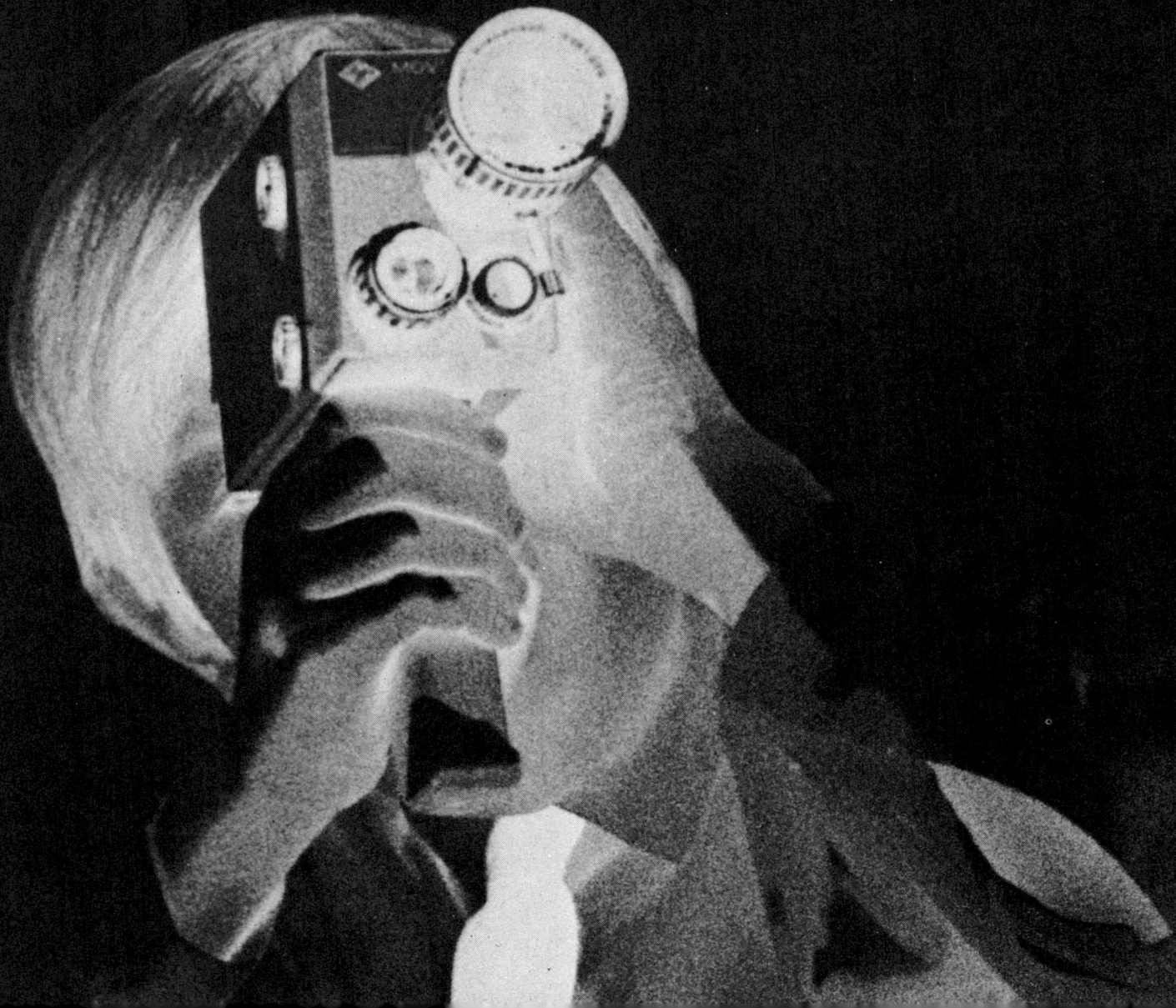

CHILDREN AS FILM MAKERS

by John Lidstone and Don McIntosh

Special photography by Roger Kerkham

VNR VAN NOSTRAND REINHOLD COMPANY

NEW YORK CINCINNATI TORONTO LONDON MELBOURNE

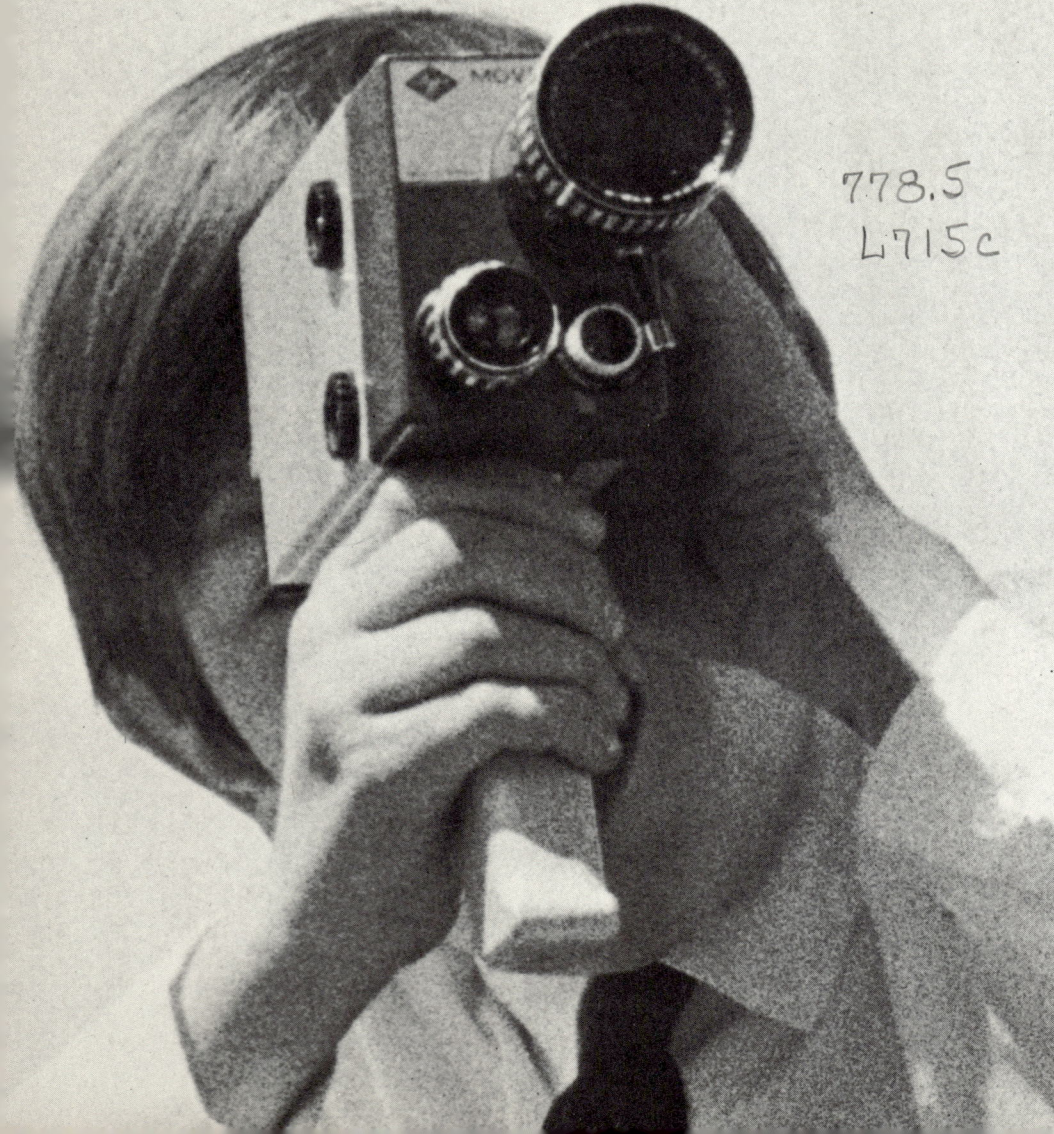

With thanks to

Colin Reed, Head, Middle School, Collegiate School, New York, and members of the Middle School Film Club. Mr. Reed's fine program in film making provided both inspiration and material for much of the book and the authors are most grateful for his cooperation.

Glen Palmer-Smith of *Sports Illustrated,* for photographs of the Collegiate Middle School Film Club.

Vera Neilson, Chatham Junior High School, Chatham, New York.

Annette Axtmann and Jana Wincenz; Agnes Russell Center, Teachers College, Columbia University, New York City.

And to Katya, Sasha, Tanya, and Lisa Kuthan; Lisa Johnson; and Elizabeth Moulden.

And especially to Dr. William Katz, Professor, School of Library Science, State University of New York at Albany, for bibliographical advice.

Van Nostrand Reinhold Company Regional Offices:
New York, Cincinnati, Chicago, Millbrae, Dallas

Van Nostrand Reinhold Company International Offices:
London, Toronto, Melbourne

72-8858

Designed by John Lidstone
Line drawings by Patrick Sean Kennedy

Published by Van Nostrand Reinhold Company,
450 West 33rd Street, New York, N.Y. 10001

Published simultaneously in Canada by
Van Nostrand Reinhold Ltd.

16 15 14 13 12 11 10 9 8 7 6 5 4 3 2

CONTENTS

CONTENTS

PREFACE

This book is designed for classroom teachers and other enthusiasts who would like to work with children in film making. It demonstrates how aesthetically worthwhile films can be created by children. It puts the technology of the school film into a proper and easily comprehended relationship to the basic and lucid ways that children express themselves. A detailed text illustrated by drawings and photographs explains the basics of camera operation, editing, splicing, animation, titling, and projection. Ways to guide children toward successful structuring of their films, methods for practical classroom organization of supplies and equipment, and ideas for the exhibition of films and the presentation of film festivals are discussed.

The book is based on the premise that the film is a varied and open-ended experience for children. It proposes that a film-making program can be a natural channel for the child's self-expression as well as an effective way to orient him to the visual age in which we live. It suggests that there is an urgent need for more and better film-making programs in the schools. Film making is approached both as an activity which can bring an excitement and a sense of accomplishment to the classroom as vital to the teacher as it is to the child, and as an art.

Film and the Child

By the time he reaches high school the average youngster will have spent countless hours in front of the TV and he will have seen literally hundreds of movies. He will not have read nearly as many books. Thus film image plays a vital part in the ongoing education of today's children —

and more and more of this "real" education is taking place outside the schools.

We who are now adults reacted, when we were children, with a hypnotic fascination to the two-dimensional magic of the "movies." There, tangibly in front of us, we found aspects of reality — light, color, and movement — that we had imagined from books. We witnessed human emotions and situations, and fantastic things such as dragons and witches, that we had experienced before through the medium of words. The children of today are reversing our pattern. They see the image first, then translate it into words. They visually know an elephant long before they read about one, because they've seen it on TV. The historical events of our time are being recalled in vivid film images rather than in words. What words can equal the film impact of a storm, the crash of a Zeppelin, or the tears on the face of a weeping woman?

The image has today become more immediate and accessible than ever before. Phenomenal advances in techniques of reproduction and transmission have enabled the graphic image to dominate magazines, billboards, newspapers, and TV. Computers and even telephones are beginning to communicate even more effectively with images than with symbols and words. In an age characterized by a revolution in visual communication the film predominates. It is the newest of the arts and yet the closest to conventional reality, for with the possible exception of animation the camera must work from the materials of actuality.

Children need little sophistication to comprehend movies. What they see on the screen is very close to what they see elsewhere. Yet the selecting and ordering of that reality can be very different from the reality that exists away from the screen. What ghetto children see in the conventional TV family show is very different from their own experience, and probably very different from the conventional middle-class family experience also. Many people deplore the vapid standards of taste and morality of popular film and TV, but they have been unable to suggest effective and practical ways to improve the quality and honesty of the media. The child sits, a passive audience, unable physically or intellectually to question and discuss the vast amount of material he sees and hears. One way to give children the chance to react with reason and judgment to films and TV is to give them a chance to make films themselves. "Learning by doing" is nowhere more appropriate than in film making. Not only do the children quickly learn the technical skills — camera techniques, lighting, directing, acting, editing, and the rest — but they also become aware of the grammar and language of films, the subjective handling of reality with which film directors, editors, cameramen, and producers have shaped our visual concepts throughout this century.

No one yet knows what can be done with films. It is a new medium. Its true nature, its extensions and limitations, are just beginning to be explored. We have used it as an extension of the stage, the novel, and even poetry. And it is in this literary context that most school English departments tend to see the film. Its documentary utility interests the historian and sociologist. The teacher of fine arts appreciates the film's ability to sensitize the student to the "elements" in art such as shape, motion, color, and contrast. Design-oriented art departments recognize the film as a valuable tool in a search for concepts and essences. We have instructional films and films concerned with emotions and reactions. The film is used for expression, exploration, and explanation. There is no one typical film just as there is no one approach to a school film program. There are as many approaches to children's films as there are differences in children. Yet somewhere inherent in the medium of film, and in all cinema-like applications of light, is a unique integral discipline. We are just beginning to understand its aesthetic and technical extensions. Perhaps this generation of children, so much of whose education is based in visual imagery, will extend the film into a truer realization of its potential.

Film and the School

Today's school finds itself in the uncomfortable position of being entrusted with the perpetuation of a culture based on the printed word at a time when the authority of the printed word is being threatened from all sides. With the impact of a new communications technology, teachers, along with everyone else, have been jolted out of the security of a word world into the uncertainty of an image world. Within a generation, "viewing" has replaced "reading" as our primary means of gaining information and forming attitudes.

Schools are products of the book era, and reading and writing are their stock in trade and will be for a long time to come, but they have not been slow in reacting to new developments. Initially, their attitude was to use the visual media to teach in more effective ways. But, most educators will admit, this has not been enough. In merely using film and television, for example, instead of becoming involved with them, neither teacher nor student comes to grips with the forces that are turning our traditional concepts of education upside down. Schools no longer want merely to share in the technological benefits of the communications revolution, they want to be part of it.

Film making is the most dynamic way, perhaps the only way, for students and teachers to become actively involved in the phenomena that are common to television and cinema, to begin to be more than passive viewers. (While the TV and film technologies may be different from each other, the *art* of the film is enough like that of television so that a knowledge of one reveals the practical and aesthetic structure of the other.) Looking at films, reading about films, discussing films, can only give one a superficial understanding. It is only in making a film that one begins to realize the possibilities of the medium.

Young film makers begin to see, to really look, through their involvement with the camera and the projector. It is never too early to encourage a youngster's development in visual sensitivity. The four- and five-year-old children shown on pages 10 and 11 are from a nursery class (at the Agnes Russell Center in Teachers College, Columbia University) that has already had some experience with both still and movie cameras. They have made slide strips, hand-worked 16mm film, and shot some animation. They have also viewed a good deal of film through loop or cartridge projectors, which they operated themselves, as well as by regular projection. The teacher, through a discussion of the viewfinder effect using folded cardboard viewers made by the children, is gently making the children aware of how amazing their classroom world looks when they stop to concentrate on it.

Closed-circuit TV has yet a different effect on a very young viewer's awareness. Just as film, a TV monitor with tapes can record the visual image and play it back at a later date. And just as in film, the TV viewer can be disconcerted by his actual appearance, which is often quite different from what he expected. Anyone who has had the shock of suddenly recognizing himself in a store-window TV display knows this feeling. In simultaneous playback this discrepancy between our self-image and actuality is augmented as the TV camera simultaneously catches our reactions. The closed-circuit TV can be set up by the school audiovisual instructor and easily operated by the students. Our children have a better chance to know themselves and their world visually than any other children in history.

The average teacher is unskilled in the craft of film making and may be apprehensive about instituting a program in a field in which he feels he is inadequate. But if he becomes involved in the *activity* of film making, he will find that it is much more a human endeavor than a technical one. While some effects in both film and television can be the result of the most advanced technology, the basic manipulation of film elements, even in a technically sophisticated film, may be no more complicated than in a film done by fourth-graders. He will discover when working with children in film that the teaching skills that stand him in good stead in other subject areas will be of far more service than any formal training in cinematography could ever be.

Working with children who create film as film is a good tonic for teachers who might otherwise have difficulty breaking loose from the literary form as a way of organizing film expression. When children are encouraged to work with film as they would with any other medium — clay, paint, wire — they are quite prepared to deal with its potentials in a very free way, exploring, discovering, and delighting in film for its own sake. The real cinematic scope of film is only just now being accepted, experimental film making having been an "underground" phenomenon for years. School films should have more in common with the efforts of the underground film makers than with commercial films if only so that students can know film as film and not as an extension of, say, the novel. Starting a new

group of film makers off scratching designs and patterns into black leader or coloring white leader with magic markers or using magic markers or inks and dyes on scrap film encourages youngsters to be experimental in all their films and bold in their conceptualizations. Considering film in this light forces us to recognize film making as a whole new field of expression.

When children are encouraged to work as naturally with film as they would with any other medium, they treat it just as another element, unique in itself and not tied by any derivative strings to any other mode of expression. In doing so, they tend to find their own creative level. This means that the teacher must accept a ten-year-old's film as such, with none of the polish of an adult film, if it is to have the honesty of expression that will mark it as significant and worthwhile. At the same time, the teacher's role is not passive. He must do far more than be accepting. Not all children are as immediately intrigued by the movie camera as one might think, and making a film requires as much hard work, organization, and persistence as any other worthwhile school project. Just as in any other classroom endeavor, the teacher must find ways of generating enthusiasm and encouraging application.

It is natural for a teacher brought up in another era to think of film making as being a complex, expensive activity with all sorts of time-consuming complications. In actuality, today's movie camera is extremely simple to operate, almost foolproof, even in the hands of very young children. Film is becoming less expensive every year and is processed in most localities within two days. The projectors and tape recorders used in school film making are designed for home use and so, once again, pose no technical problems. Editors and splicers, too, have been simplified to the point where children can use them with no trouble. Older children often want to express themselves through involved techniques but are usually so sophisticated in the cinematic processes that they can handle the technical complexities themselves and, in any case, do not expect the teacher to have all the answers. Invariably, individuals and groups will work in areas in which they feel confident, so that a film-making project seldom gets out of hand in this regard. When it seems time to expand a program technically, it is wise to seek outside help. Once one becomes involved in film making it is amazing the number of contacts one makes in the field, and it is never difficult to get out-of-school help for a program. Most film programs encourage group and individual activities to run side by side. In such cases, it is often advantageous to have interested teachers in the school along with interested adult film makers to serve as tutors to work with students making their own films. When a program has been in existence for two or three years, advanced film makers from the group might take over this responsibility and assist new members.

Film making, while a subject area in its own right, is also the means to other ends. By engaging children in an activity in which each participant must pull his own weight if the group's purposes are to be achieved, a film program can involve children in realistic social situations. In encouraging a youngster to use a camera out of school it brings him into a confrontation with his environment in a way that makes him dramatically aware of its qualities and alert to its problems. It introduces him, too, to an aesthetic ordering of elements consistent with contemporary expression and gives him an in-depth understanding of the manipulative dimension of film, thereby educating his taste in the visual media. It heightens his appreciation of both telvision and the cinema; and, as a side benefit, in his work with sound tracks, it makes him a more sensitive listener to recorded sound, both music and speech.

The success of a film-making program is dependent on the soundness of its organization. The first consideration might be what form the program will take in school. For example, until recently it has been a club activity in most schools, inspired by the enthusiasm of an interested teacher. Now, film making as an established program is becoming part of the curriculum of more and more elementary and secondary schools. In most schools where film making has been introduced it has rapidly become so popular that a casual program cannot cope with the large numbers of students who want to participate, with the unfortunate result that many youngsters never get the opportunity to benefit from a film-making experience. Space must be set aside, not only for working, but for the storage of equipment. Keeping equipment in order and checking it in and out can become a film-making instructor's nightmare unless this aspect of the program is well thought out and adequate space is provided. Some sort of budget needs to be set before the first session of the group, as funds will be needed in the first week that film is shot. Film making does not lend itself to a series of regular classroom meetings. Teachers who work this way soon find themselves forced into an academic pattern involving film study, reaction papers, and so on, which has little to do with the dynamics of active film making. A looser structure sustained by group projects, such as organizing a film library, presenting noon-hour film shows, writing a film journal, preparing for a film festival of student films, and, of course, some social events, an evening of unusual films, a visit to a film studio, is perhaps the best way of maintaining a tight group structure but a relaxed laboratory situation where both group and individual work can go on. Film making as a classroom activity nevertheless has a great potential, particularly in the early grades, where animation, for example, can be carried on with a single camera

and organizational detail reduced to a minimum. If teachers of the various subject areas encourage their students to use films for research and for reportage and eventually present them in the classroom, film making will be an active part of school life. The art teacher might be approached to act as the consultant for parts of films, such as titles and animated sequences that involve the use of art materials. Arrangements should be made for both students and staff to move freely in and out of school; releases signed by parents should be received as soon as school opens, and the administration should be informed of the necessity of students shooting outside the school.

Who should teach film making in school? At this stage in the development of school film making, this is a difficult question to answer. In any case, it is perhaps more useful to discuss how film making should be taught rather than who should teach it. Quite decidedly, it should not be presented as a technical subject and it should not become merely an extension of a specific area such as art or English. Whoever teaches film making must conceive of it as a unique form of expression, even though it may be thought of as an art or as a form of communication or as the matrix of a number of expressive forces.

There must be an empathy, too, with the enthusiasms and aspirations of the young film maker and a deep appreciation of the unique qualities of his films. The experienced film maker who knows all about films but nothing about children would be a poor substitute for the experienced teacher without a film to his credit but full of enthusiasm and understanding. In this visual age, we are all much more sophisticated about film than we realize, and once in the swing of film making, we are soon much more at home than we ever imagined we would be. In the final analysis, every teacher is a potential film maker and teacher of film making, and every classroom a studio.

THE CAMERA AND HOW TO USE IT

When to Start Shooting

Using the camera itself is the aspect of film making that usually appeals most to youngsters. Their enthusiasm is never at a higher level than when they set out to shoot their first reels of film. Take advantage of this initial eagerness. Have the students shooting just as soon as they understand how to handle a camera. The modern 8mm and Super 8 cameras with automatic light meters and simplified focusing are so easy to run that there is no reason why actual filming cannot take place the first day a film club or class meets. Don't stifle the students' enthusiasm with too many preliminaries. Help them to find their own way, work toward freshness and spontaneity; more advanced techniques can come later. In a school where cameras are scarce a child might only have the opportunity to shoot a few feet of film with the school camera; in another school each youngster might have a camera of his own for a day or two.

Some teachers of film making advocate beginning with still cameras or with viewings and discussions of examples of good film making. These are pale substitutes for working on one's own with a loaded movie camera. Preparatory activities that postpone the actual shooting detract from the sharp edge of excitement that is so important if children are to make inventive and sensitive films.

The one disadvantage of film making as an art experience for children is the time lapse between shooting and viewing the developed film. However, one-day or two-day developing services are often available, making it possible for students to view their films while the shooting experience is still fresh in their minds.

It is wise, perhaps, to structure to a certain extent the first shooting experiences of a film class. Some students will already have a subject in mind and will proceed without further encouragement, the teacher giving technical advice and consoling the student when he overreaches his proficiency. Most of the students, however, will appreciate the security and motivation of a common assigned subject, one that lends itself to a variety of interpretations. This has several advantages. No one is at a loss trying to decide what to do; the class discovers through its own work that there are many ways of looking at the same thing; the shooting produces a great deal of footage with a common theme, which can be used to good effect in the first session on editing; and the class is confronted with tangible evidence — since the same visual material is sure to be shot by more than one person — that certain simple techniques, such as holding the camera steady and panning slowly, render satisfactory images, while misuse of the camera results in disappointments. The class can decide on a theme popular with everyone and each individual can be encouraged to interpret it in his own way. In the lower grades attention could be directed toward a subject easily treated within the classroom or perhaps be an animation project involving a fixed camera. In the upper grades it is worth considering more challenging topics such as "space" or "motion" or "feet" or "communication" or even "the female of the species" or "water and wind." Another alternative for the first shooting experience is filming at a specific location if the neighborhood has any visually exciting possibilities such as an airport, a zoo, or an auto junkyard.

Selecting a Camera

Three kinds of cameras are generally used in school film making: the 16mm, the 8mm, and the Super 8. 16mm film making is expensive and rarely practical for a school group, and little space has been devoted to it in this book. However, the bibliography includes books for those who are interested in 16mm.

The best camera to use depends on the type of film making planned and the age of the children. A camera used for animation, for example, should have special features such as a single-frame release and lenses that focus very close to the subject. A camera that is just right for a fourth-grade group might be unsuitable for an eighth-grade camera club with considerable film-making experience.

It is worth taking time to try out possible cameras in the class situation before purchase. It is often possible to rent a given camera for a school term or less from a local dealer and to buy it later at a discount should it prove to be the camera you want.

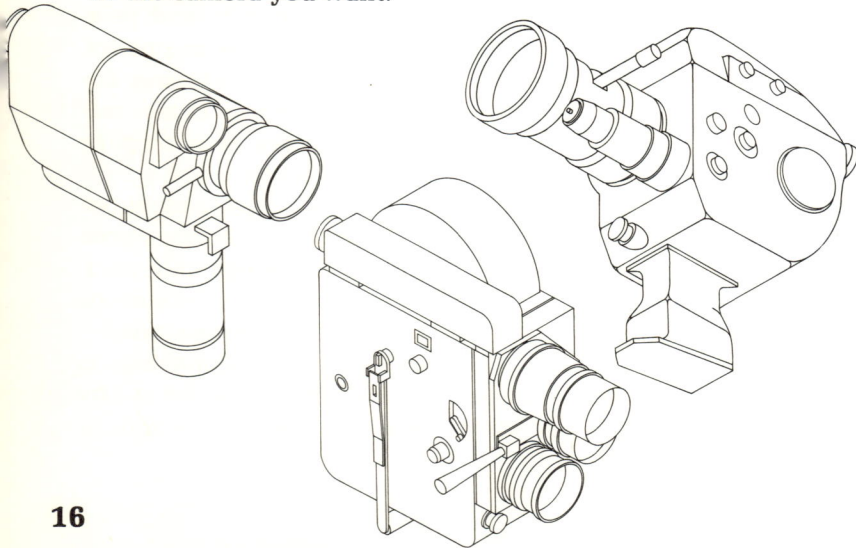

In most cases the following are desirable features to look for in any 8mm or Super 8 camera:

1. Power and/or manual zoom lens. (Different cameras have different zoom ranges. Given an equal quality of lens, the better cameras are the ones with longer ranges, giving a ratio between telephoto and close-up of about five to one. This provides more flexibility than the more common three-to-one ratio.)
2. Built-in automatic light meter exposure with manual override.
3. Split-image or other aid for focusing through the lens.
4. Single-lens-reflex viewfinder.
5. Single-frame exposure release and cable release.
6. Battery-powered film drive with different speeds (usually 12, 18, and 24 frames per second).
7. Footage counter.
8. Battery check.
9. Carry case.
10. Instruction manual.

If the camera is to be used in interview or theatrical situations then "sync" systems are desirable.

A school with funds for equipment can find suitable cameras for almost any situation. On the other hand, many good school programs have begun with little more equipment than the teacher's own 8mm camera or a Bolex 16mm donated by an interested parent. Additional cameras soon turn up, a result of the enthusiasm engendered by both student and teacher. Most camera shops have many second-hand 8mm cameras cluttering up their back shelves. Some of these are excellent and are available at very reasonable prices. It is also well to bear in mind that sometimes the less expensive camera is simpler to operate and more suitable for children.

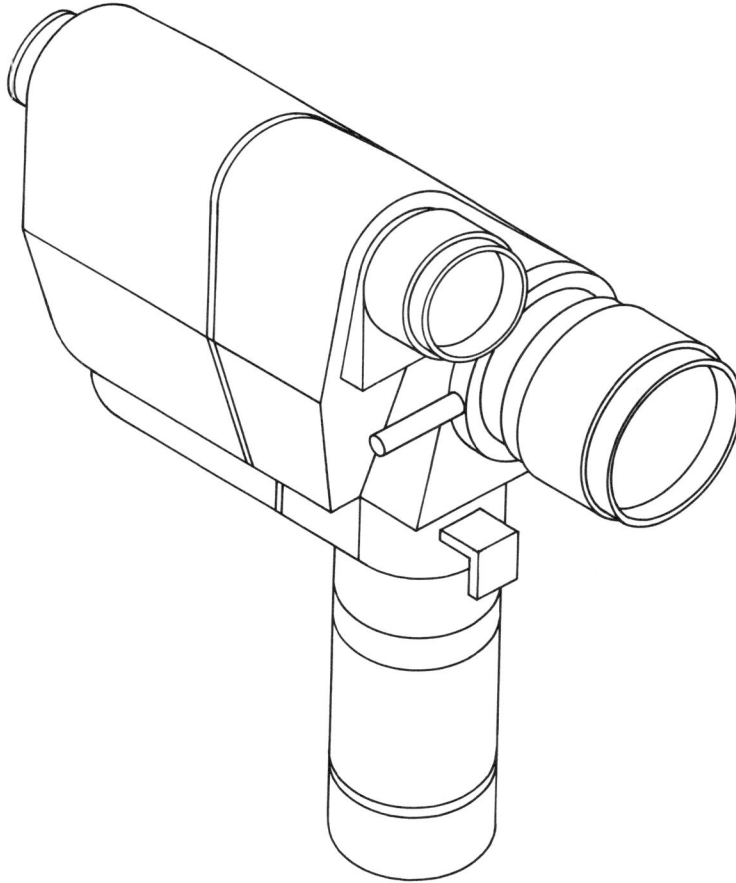

8mm

Advantages:

Because 8mm film is wound on an open reel instead of packaged in a sealed cassette, a length of film can be exposed to give background images, then wound back so that other images can be superimposed. For example, title letters filmed against a black background (which allows the color potential of the film to remain active) can be shown superimposed over an image background when the film is wound back again and reshot.

Because Super 8 equipment has become so popular with the home-movie maker, 8mm cameras and projectors, both new and second hand, are available at low prices and may even be donated by parents who have switched to Super 8. Some of these have built-in features that are available only on the more expensive Super 8's. 8mm film splicers, editors, and other accessories are still easy to obtain.

Disadvantages:

8mm film is just as expensive as Super 8 but projects a smaller image. Also, 8mm film has a double set of images on it and is split down the center in processing; thus its reels must be flipped in shooting and so some frames are often lost and shooting time is wasted, often at an important point in a film.

8mm equipment is being phased out by most companies so that new cameras are hard to get and film, repairs, and service may become difficult to obtain (although this does not apply at the present time). The film may take longer to be processed, although only in smaller communities.

As 8mm film comes on an open reel instead of in a closed cassette with built-in exposure controls it can be more easily light-struck and incorrectly exposed.

Super 8mm

Advantages:

Super 8 film and equipment is easily available. Fifty feet of film can be shot without the inconvenience of flipping reels. The film is no more expensive then 8mm and projects a much larger image. It is easier to see in the editor, making editing simpler.

All advances in small-camera technology are being made in Super 8. Super 8 film comes in light-tight cassettes that are easy to use and automatically set the exposure index. They do not have to be handled, once installed in the camera, until the film is used up.

Disadvantages:

As it is impossible to rewind the cartridges on Super 8, double-exposure effects and superimposition of titles on film action are not possible. (However, the Fujica "single 8" system, which projects an image as large as Super 8, does have the rewind feature.)

Super 8 equipment may cost a school more than 8mm, because donations of cameras and projectors are less likely and inexpensive second-hand equipment is not generally available.

Some of the extra-sophisticated devices that are available on inexpensive 8mm cameras are only found on more expensive Super 8 cameras (at present).

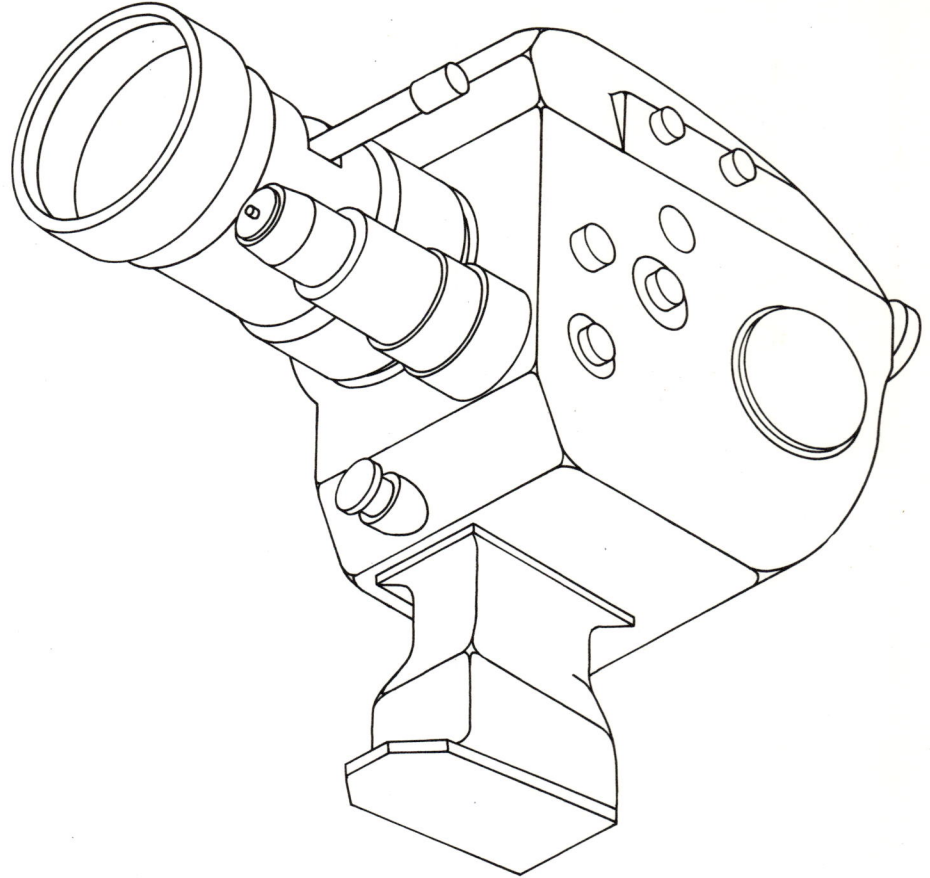

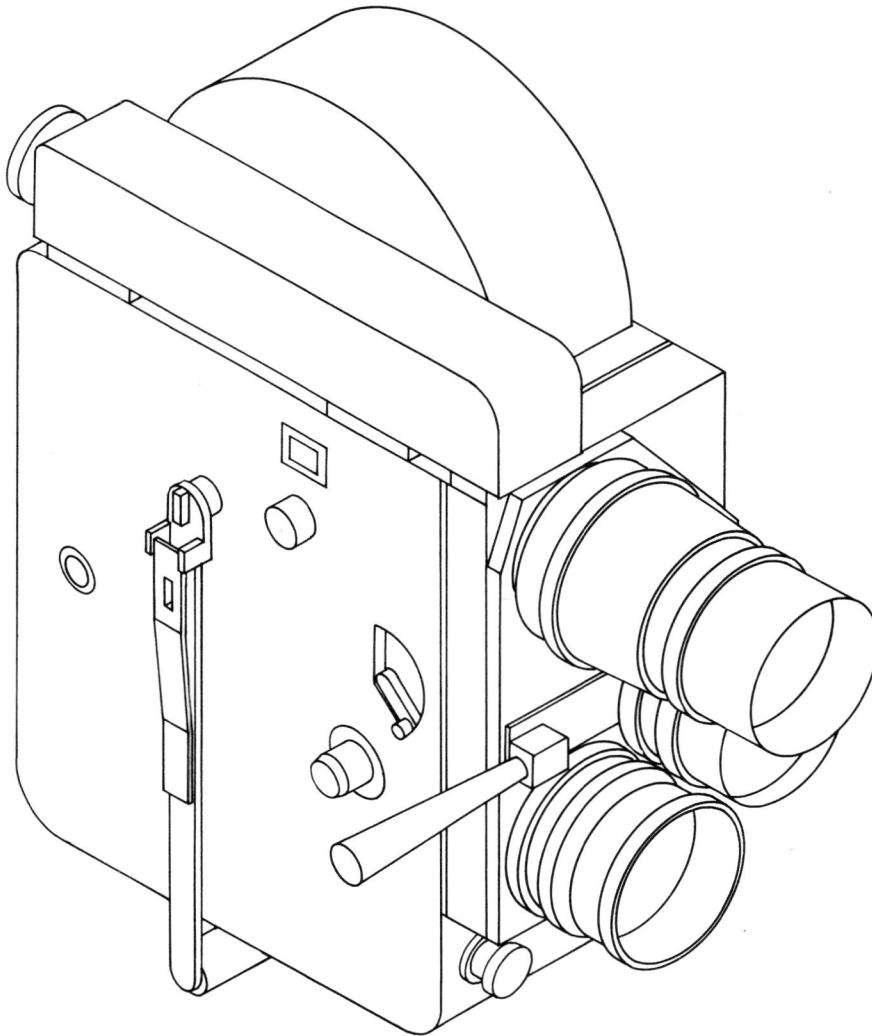

16mm

Advantages:

Large-scale projection is sharper than with 8mm and Super 8. The film is easier to edit and splice, and laboratory services for special effects are geared to it.

The 16mm camera has a wide range of lenses, speeds, and technical devices, and lends itself to superimposition, dissolves, and fades. The sound quality is better and easier to synchronize. The camera itself is rugged and built for hard use.

16mm has commercial possibilities on TV and in theaters and schools.

Disadvantages:

All 16mm equipment and services are much more expensive than 8mm and Super 8.

The camera is more complicated to use and does not lend itself as well to spontaneous shooting; it is heavy for children to handle.

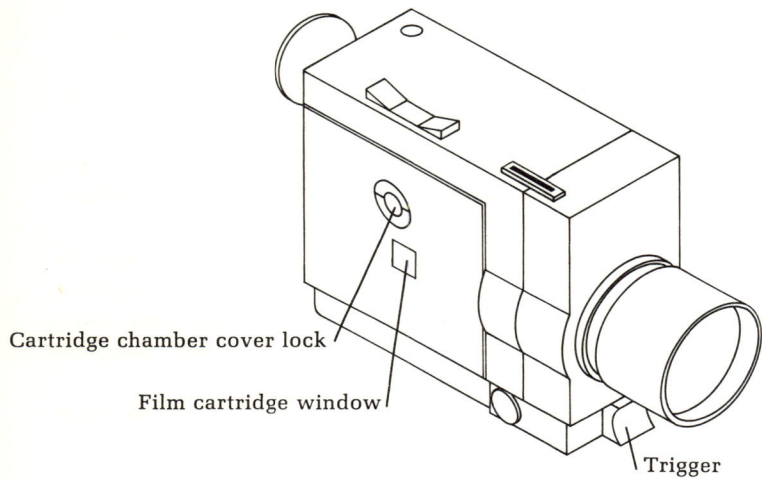

Cartridge chamber cover lock

Film cartridge window

Trigger

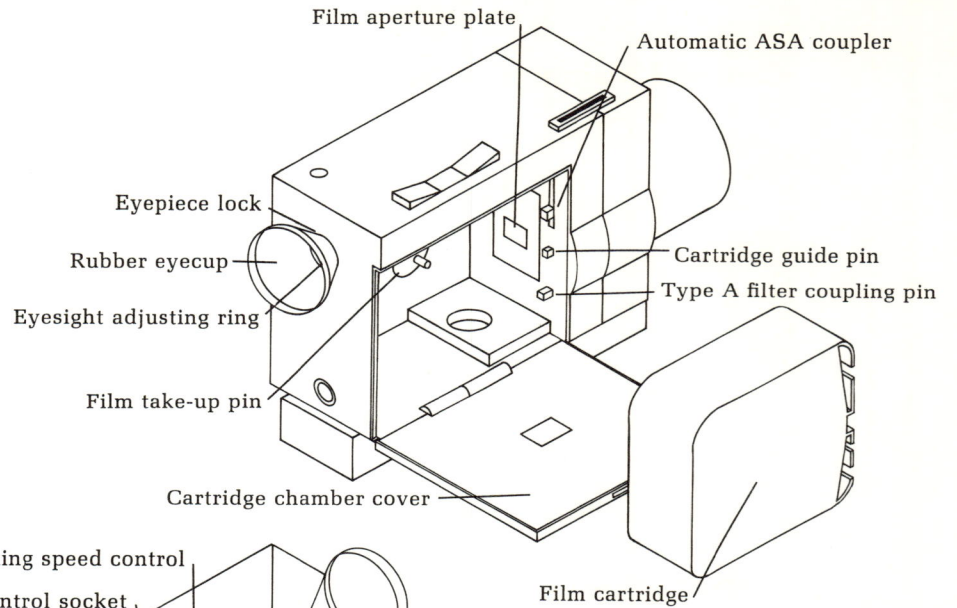

Film aperture plate

Automatic ASA coupler

Eyepiece lock

Rubber eyecup

Eyesight adjusting ring

Cartridge guide pin

Type A filter coupling pin

Film take-up pin

Cartridge chamber cover

Film cartridge

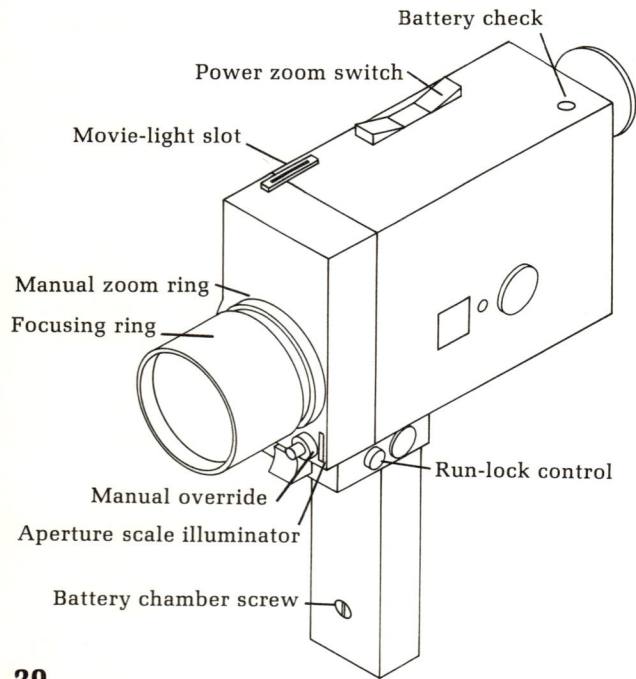

Battery check

Power zoom switch

Movie-light slot

Manual zoom ring

Focusing ring

Manual override

Aperture scale illuminator

Battery chamber screw

Run-lock control

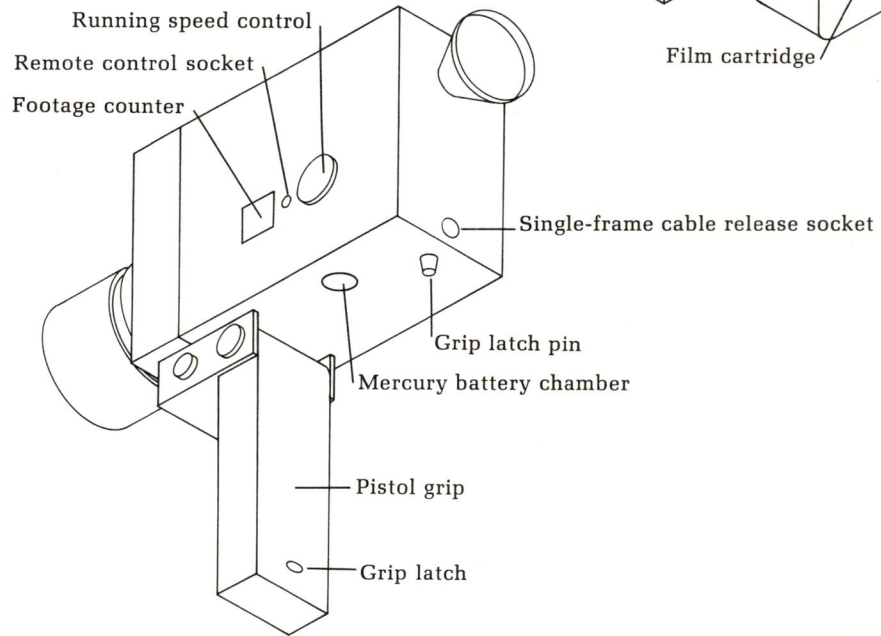

Running speed control

Remote control socket

Footage counter

Single-frame cable release socket

Grip latch pin

Mercury battery chamber

Pistol grip

Grip latch

Care and Maintenance of the Camera

Most movie cameras are remarkably strong and durable. They will cheerfully endure the average stresses and strains of a school program. Should any mechanical defect occur, however, the camera should be returned to the dealer or maker for repair. It is far too complex an instrument for the student or teacher to work on.

Everyday care and maintenance are very simple. The following points are important:

1. Each camera should have its own carry case. Cardboard containers and foam insulation soon deteriorate under constant use. A leather case with a shoulder strap and pockets for camera accessories is usually not expensive.

2. When not in use the camera should be stored inside its carry case. The mercury battery in the light meter will, of course, last much longer (up to a year or two) if the camera is stored in the dark. Temperatures in the storage area should be moderate and the humidity low. It is very unwise to "cook" the camera by keeping it in direct sunlight, inside a car for example, or to encourage mold and rust by storing it in a damp cupboard. It is important to remove the motor-drive batteries and the mercury light-meter batteries during storage for any long period of time, as corrosion can affect delicate parts of the camera. Film also deteriorates and should not be stored in the camera over long periods. As a general rule it should be developed as soon as shot.

3. Even when the camera is in constant use the batteries should be checked each day before shooting. Many cameras have two-way battery-check switches, and if there is any doubt about the batteries it is best to replace them at once. The child whose best shots have been lost through battery failure will be very disappointed; it is better to be overcautious. Alkaline energizer batteries are much better than the older penlight batteries, which could power only three to five cartridges. A spare set of these batteries for the motor drive and power zoom should be kept in the carry case. The mercury battery that powers the automatic light meter should last up to a year or more in regular use, but if exposure problems are encountered the fault should generally be first checked for here.

4. The camera should be cleaned very infrequently and only when absolutely necessary. Most camera interiors are tightly closed and are opened only to insert film. If care is taken during the loading, little dust will be admitted. If the camera must be cleaned, then a blower brush or soft camel-hair brush can be used. A lens tissue can be used on the film aperture, but nothing harder, as the fine polished surface can be scratched and scratches will be transferred to the film. The lens is even more delicate. Always keep the lens cap on when the camera is not being used. The lens should never be touched with the fingers, as the body acid can eat into the special emulsion with which most lens are coated. The blower brush can be used to remove dust from the lens. Special lens tissue and in severe cases a lens-cleaning fluid can be used to remove grime, but facial tissues or handkerchiefs should never be used; they will scratch the lens surface or leave lint.

5. Like any other modern technical instrument, the mechanism of the camera should never be forced. A child should be made aware that if some stiffness occurs or if one part does not fit into another, the fault probably lies in the operator. The child should consult the camera manual or the teacher.

Loading the Camera

8mm and 16mm cameras are usually loaded by threading the film through the camera gate from a loaded spool to the empty take-up spool. The loading should be done in subdued light, and the full reel must be held carefully to prevent the coiled film from unwinding. Most 8mm cameras have a threading diagram on the floor of the magazine. As an added aid, 8mm spools have a three-slotted center hole on one side and a four-slotted aperture on the other. When inserting the spools on the capstans, the slots are matched with the fins on the bottom of the capstans. The take-up spool, for example, nearly empty at the beginning, is placed with the four slots down matching the four fins at the base of the motor capstan. After the film has been threaded from the full reel at the top of the camera through the film-gate aperture to the take-up spool, make sure that the gate is closed and the film counter set. Then run the film briefly to make sure it is threaded correctly. This will expose some film, but approximately ten seconds are clipped off the film in developing anyway. If the film is moving through the aperture normally, close the magazine and run off the remainder of the ten seconds of waste film. The first half of raw film is now set for shooting.

The procedures for loading and for changing the reels in an 8 mm camera are described step by step on pages 24-25. Steps 6-12 are the same for both loading and changing.

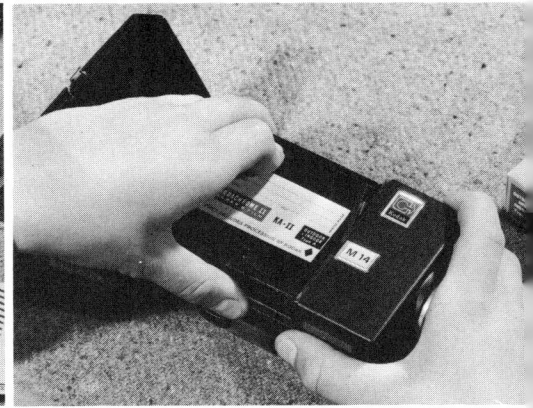

Super 8 cameras are much easier to load. The whole 50 feet of film is enclosed in a light-tight cassette, which is inserted under a guide pin at the film aperture and press clipped into the magazine. The magazine is then closed and latched. The insertion of the cassette automatically sets the film counter, the ASA reading, and the Type A filter-coupling pin.

Top: Positioning a cassette in a side-loading Super 8 camera.
Bottom: Positioning a cassette in an end-loading Super 8 camera.

Changing 8mm Reels

1. Open magazine when first half of film has been run off.

2. Remove loaded spool.

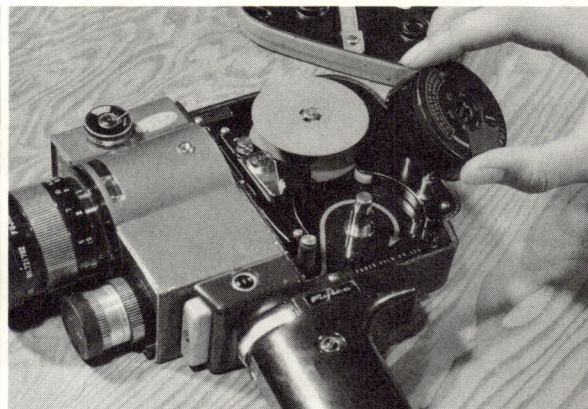

3. Be careful to keep film from unwinding.

7. Thread film along channel, following diagram on floor of magazine.

8. Close gate (in some cameras also apply film counter) to keep film in place.

9. Thread film on empty spool, which now has three slots facing up.

4. Tighten up loose coils and turn over spool so three-slotted center hole is on bottom.

5. Remove empty reel and open gate.

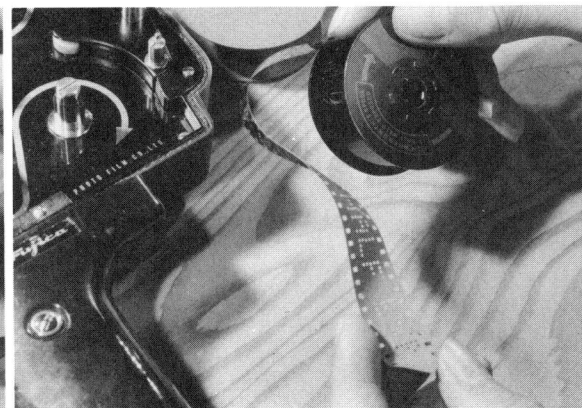

6. Pull out a length of film for threading. (Note when reel is reversed, first section has "HALF EXP" written on it.)

10. Tighten up coils of film.

11. Insert reel on bottom post, making sure slots are firmly fixed on capstan. Run camera briefly to be sure film flows freely.

12. Close case and lock. Run off remainder of ten seconds of waste film.

Handling and Shooting the Camera

When they have the opportunity to shoot sufficient film, children soon use the camera with an unself-conscious mastery. Through experience and experiment the camera often becomes so familiar to the student that he uses it naturally and fluently as an extension of his mind and body. Adults are usually amazed at how quickly youngsters can acquire the discipline of effective camera technique. Teachers are often just as surprised by the inventive and exciting innovations in film shooting discovered by their students. The young film maker may dangle the camera on a rope to simulate the feeling of someone hanging, he may attach the camera to his bike and film his journey in single-frame releases, timed one second apart, or he may reroll and double-expose the image of a slide of a building projected on the actual building at night. His mind is young and fertile, already familiar with today's technological innovations.

While children should be encouraged to use the camera creatively, they should also be cautioned that too many special effects can result in a distracting and boring film. Good camera technique furthers the intent of the film. Agitated or blurred camera work caused either by inexperience in shooting or by too much concern with camera gimmicks will cause a viewer to lose concentration in a movie and distract him from whatever the film maker is trying to say. Steady and unobtrusive camerawork often is the best policy for school films.

Except for animation, most shooting by children will be done with the camera hand-held. Cameras with pistol grips are the most convenient to handle and make it easier for a youngster to maintain a firm hold. Most people shoot

right-handed and right-eyed, and whatever the design of the camera, the supporting arm should be held firmly against the body and the camera cradled against the cheekbone or forehead. The right hand usually takes the weight of the camera while the left hand steadies it from above and is in a position to operate controls for the zoom lens, the focus, the manual light settings, the camera speed, etc. Both hands must be positioned so as not to interfere with the lens or cover up the electric eye of the light meter.

Shooting a camera is very much like. shooting a gun. The firmest and the most comfortable kind of support is desirable. The camera operator should be neither too tense and strained nor too careless and loose. Many experienced cameramen interrupt their breathing at the moment of shooting just as does the rifle marksman.

For panning (a continuous movement of the camera while shooting) the feet should be planted firmly apart and the body swung from the hips so that the body acts as a tripod. Using a natural support to steady the camera, for example by resting it on a fence or leaning it against a tree trunk or wall corner, helps to prevent unnecessarily jerky sequences. Particular care must be taken when using the extended zoom range or a telescopic lens, because the greater the distance, the more noticeable "camera shake" will be.

As a general rule it is wise to shoot sequences too long rather than too short. It takes the viewer longer than the camera operator to identify the subject, and besides it is always much easier to edit a long sequence than to reshoot a short one. The beginning student should perhaps count slowly to five or seven when depressing the camera trigger to get a feel for the best length for the average shot ("one thousand and one, one thousand and two," etc.).

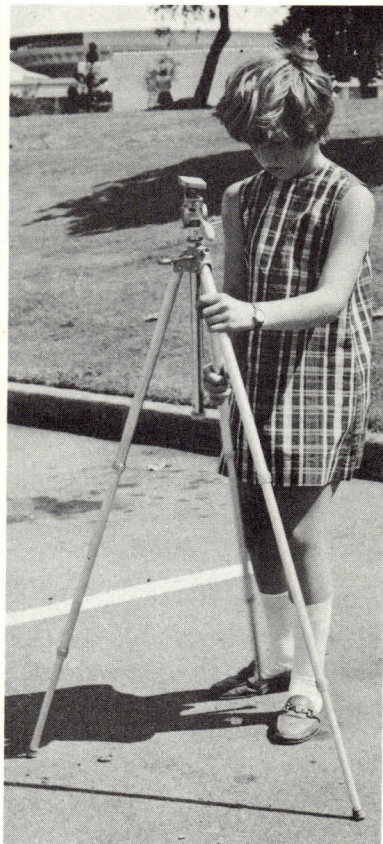

The Tripod

For stable camerawork it is best to use a tripod. With the camera fixed to an immovable base the threat of a jumpy image is practically eliminated. When purchasing a tripod make sure that it has a movie head, so that the camera can scan in any direction, and a side tilt to make attaching the camera easier. One should test the maneuverability of the head with a camera attached to be sure the weight of the camera doesn't hinder it. A cheap tripod with legs like fishing poles is worse than useless for student film making. The student needs a sturdy yet portable support. Monopods, with only one leg instead of three, are handy when the camera has to be moved quickly, and slings, into which the monopods can be inserted, make cameramen even more mobile, but, because of the extra cost, they are seldom used in school film making.

While the tripod is an effective stabilizer, it has its hazards. Children must know how to extend the legs and how to adjust them to accommodate the tripod to flat and hilly terrain. They have to understand just what to tighten and loosen so that the head will travel the way they want it to. If just one catch or screw is unadjusted, the tripod may collapse or the camera may freeze in the wrong position at a crucial moment. Children should gain some experience in adjusting the tripod and attaching the camera before they go out on their own.

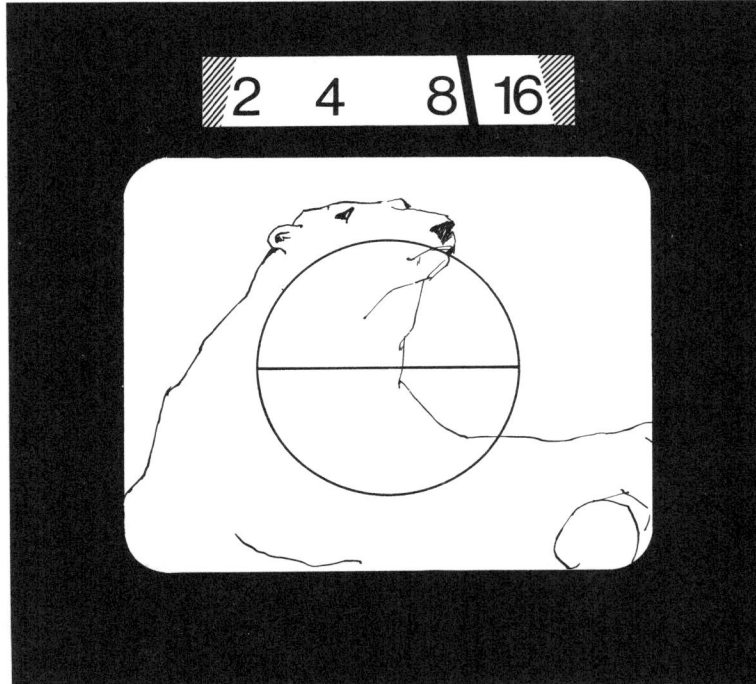

Exposure

Almost all modern 8mm and Super 8 cameras have a fully automatic exposure system. This equips the camera to take a reading of the available light on the subject and to set the lens aperture to the appropriate stop, an automatic operation that greatly simplifies the cameraman's job. If there is insufficient light or too much light for a good exposure on the film, the camera signals the operator. In some older cameras or in less expensive cameras, an indicator such as a colored flag, usually yellow, will appear in the viewfinder. In other cameras a calibrated scale is located in an aperture, usually adjacent to the view finder, with a needle that indicates what lens opening the automatic exposure system has selected. If the needle swings anywhere between F/1.8 (the white area just before "2") and F/16, the light is all right and the exposure will be correct. If, however, the needle dips into the red flag on the left, the light is insufficient and a faster film, a slower camera filming speed, or an artificial light is needed. On the other hand, if the needle swings into the right-hand flag there is too much light. The remedy here is a less sensitive film, a faster shooting speed, or a neutral-density filter. In most cameras, depressing the camera trigger to the first tension position activates the light meter without starting the camera's motor, permitting any adjustment before the film is exposed. In some cameras the light meter will not work until the film is loaded, and other cameras have a switch that disconnects the light meter, thus preserving the mercury batteries.

Manual Override. Most cameras have a manual override on the automated light meter. The manual override is a must for single-frame releases and animation (discussed on pages 76-84). It is also very useful in compensating for the inadequacy of the automatic light meter exposure system. The light meter tends to read the surrounding light in the immediate environment of the camera. If, for example, the cameraman is standing in the deep shade of trees, filming a subject in a sunlit meadow, the camera, having sensed the diminished light of the shadows, will have opened the lens aperture so that an extended zoom shot of the meadow will be greatly overexposed. The solution is to walk over and take a reading near the subject in the meadow on the automatic light meter, say F/8, switch the meter to M for manual and hand-set the needle to F/8, then return to the shadow of the trees for the shot. The same procedure applies to the shooting of the features of a face on a sunwashed beach or on a glistening snow field. Trees and buildings, when shot against the clear sky, need manual adjustment or else they become silhouetted.

Film Speed and Lighting. There is a very limited selection of film speeds in 8mm and Super 8. Black-and-white film is generally a faster film and can be used in situations where there is less light available. Black-and-white film, being less popular than color, is harder to find, and developing takes two or three times as long. Whatever the type of film used in 8mm cameras, the ASA setting on the film container must be checked and the camera set accordingly. Super 8 cassettes, as has been noted, set the ASA coupling pin automatically upon insertion.

Film designed for daylight use and film designed for use with photofloods are available in 8mm. Black-and-white film is also easier to obtain in 8mm than in Super 8. 8mm indoor film (photoflood) can be used for outdoor filming with the attachment of a Type A filter #85. Another filter of this type should also be attached to the light-meter aperture if it is separate from the photo lenses.

Most of the Super 8 color film available from camera shops and film dealers is tungsten-balanced Type A film, and most Super 8 cameras are equipped with Type A fil-

ters in position for outdoor shooting. No adjustment is necessary until artificial light is used. When photofloods or movie lights are used, the filter must be swung out of the light path. This is usually accomplished by the use of a key or pin inserted into a slot marked for that purpose. (Students tend to lose these keys if they are not attached somehow to the camera.) In the case of Super 8 movie lights this key is often part of the attachment and the light can be fixed directly to the camera with it. In other cameras a bracket is attached for a single movie light or brace of lights. This lighting is adequate for most movies, although it is important that subjects stand fairly close to a wall or some other reflecting surface so that they are not spotlighted against the dark. For portraits and similar compositions a better method of lighting that brings out the three-dimensionality of the subject is still the conventional arrangement of two free-standing photofloods set at the same or higher level and slightly behind the camera on either side and striking the subject at a 45-degree angle. With this type of lighting, however, the subject must remain within a very restricted area. For more natural and freer action, movie lights or photofloods can be "bounced" off white or light walls and ceilings for more pleasant and natural lighting if those surfaces are near enough to the subject. Photofloods and movie lights have a short life and get very hot. They should be turned on for brief periods only and great care should be taken with them. It is wise to avoid lights with exposed bulbs when working with young children. The sealed-beam type of movie light is usually safer.

Camera Speed. Some cameras have adjustable filming speeds, any of which the student can select. The standard silent speed is 18 frames per second, and 24 frames per second is the speed recommended when sound will be striped on the film (see pages 72-75). The more frames per second, the faster the camera runs and the slower the motion will appear to be on the developed film. A speed of 12 frames per second will give a jerky, comic, quick action similar to early movies. The Super 8 camera automatic exposure system is keyed to the speed selector and it automatically compensates when the filming speed is changed. Most 8mm and Super 8 cameras have a single-frame release socket. A cable release can be inserted into the socket and then each time the plunger is extended one frame of film will be exposed. This is a useful feature for animation and special effects in film making, and it is discussed on pages 79-84. The light meter must be on a manual setting when using the single-frame release.

Filters. The limited and simplified use of filters in 8mm and Super 8 film making should reassure any anxious teacher or student. There is practically no filter problem in the normal use of the Super 8 camera. The simple insertion of a key or pin shifts the daylight filter and enables the camera to operate with artificial light. Regular 8mm cameras can be loaded with daylight film for daylight shooting or indoor film for artificial light so that no filter is necessary. Conversion filters can be purchased to attach to 8mm cameras if desired. The Fujika single-8 system, for example, has a daylight filter for both light meter and lens as an accessory. Other types of filters for unusual effects can also be obtained. Advanced students may wish to produce color reversals, film molten glass or metal, and so on, but such exotic projects requiring special filters are not usually undertaken by students.

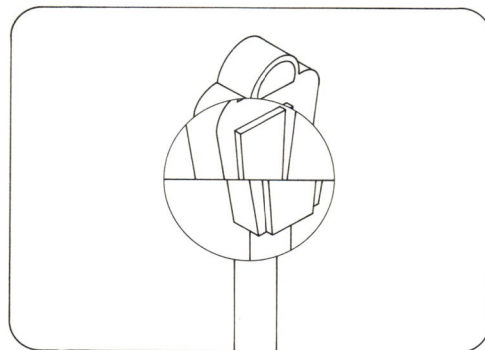

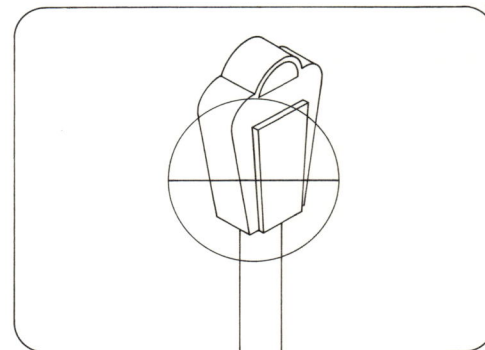

Focusing

Children have little trouble learning how to focus, although they do sometimes forget to focus before shooting. It is important to make focusing a definite step in filming procedure and to encourage students to check the focus just before pressing the trigger.

Since most 8mm and Super 8 cameras today have a zoom lens, this discussion will use the zoom lens as an example, although the same principles apply to any lens.

Modern 8mm and Super 8 cameras are nearly all reflex cameras. This means that the actual viewing for focusing is seen — by the help of a system of prisms — through the same lens through which the film is exposed. This greatly simplifies camera operation, especially for closeups, as the student knows that he will be filming exactly what he sees in the viewfinder. (This is not true of the parallax system, in which the viewfinder shows an image slightly shifted due to the parallel but separate installation of the viewfinder lens and the camera lens; the student must remember to compensate, particularly in closeups.) A reflex movie camera usually has two lenses to adjust. The first adjustments should be made in the eyepiece lens. This will not directly affect the focus in the camera but will coordinate the lens to the particular cameraman's eye. The focus ring is turned to infinity (∞) and the student lines up a distant view and then adjusts the rangefinder image by turning the eyesight adjusting ring until the image appears sharp. He then locks the eyesight ring in that position by turning an eyepiece lock and the camera is now set to his personal vision. The camera must be reset when another student uses it.

The following procedure for focusing should be followed in teaching students to focus the zoom lens.

1. "Zoom up" or extend the lens fully out to its telephoto position, because the shallowest depth of field is obtained at this position and the sharpest focus is required.
2. Rotate the focusing ring to get the sharpest image or until the split images appear continuous and unbroken.
3. Zoom lens back until the desired field is covered. If the focus is fixed in the extended telephoto position, the camera will remain in focus throughout the length of the zoom.
4. Refocus every time you move or change camera position.

Not all cameras have blurred-image or split-image focus, but these types of focus are the most common and the easiest, generally speaking, for the students to work with. Whatever the system, the camera should have a simply written manual explaining the device the camera uses for focus.

The students who use the camera will quickly become familiar with its particular method. Some inexpensive cameras even have a fixed focus so that everything is in focus unless the camera is too close to an object (usually five or six feet). Other cameras, such as the new Bell and Howell, work something like a surveyor's instrument, using gravity and trigonometry to control the focus automatically. All systems are easily mastered by children once they have had experience with the camera.

Zooming

Children are captivated by the zoom lens and will invariably want a camera with one, if they have a choice. The zoom lens incorporates a complete transition from wide angle through normal to telephoto. It can give the impression of a dolly shot, moving in or out of the area of a subject without actually moving the camera. It will permit the student to shoot subjects such as animals in their cages or people deep in conversation from a distance without interfering with their naturalness. The student can frame his composition aesthetically in the viewfinder without dashing back and forth to get the right focal length. Students using turret-lens cameras or other cameras without zoom lenses must interrupt their filming to change lenses and then refocus. The student using the zoom lens captures all the action desired without refocusing while moving from wide angle to the telephoto lens.

However, children tend to overuse the zoom lens. They love the pulsating effect of a quick series of zooms, and this can be very distracting to the viewer. While a slow zoom on occasion is undeniably dramatic, constant zooming can be boring. Students should be cautioned to use the power zoom sparingly.

The camera should be firmly held, usually in a tripod, for body shake is very noticeable when zooming. The manual zoom is most useful in setting the lens in a desired position between its telephoto and wide-angle extremities for pleasant frame-filling compositions. In shooting quick action it is often difficult to go through the time-consuming routine for focusing described above. It is possible to use the manual zoom ring to select the composition quickly and then to focus at that lens position, but no further zoom changes should be attempted without refocusing.

Special Effects

Children quickly discover the camera's capacity to achieve special visual effects that startle the viewer into new perceptions of his world. For example, shooting reflections in water or mirrors or filming refractions in raindrops or in cut glass soon become part of their film discoveries. The use of color filters or color light can also suggest new possibilities.

Special effects are useful in making transitions between one film sequence and another. A simple method of passing from one scene to another is to rotate the focus ring so that the camera goes completely out of focus, then to start the next sequence by bringing the camera slowly into focus on the next scene. This usually suggests in film language a change of time or locale. The "wipe" has a similar purpose. A simple way for the student to wipe is to pass a piece of black nonreflecting cardboard (TV board) in front of the camera lens from left to right until it blocks the whole field. The next shot can begin by slowly removing the card from in front of the lens. The "fade-out" can be achieved in a crude way by encircling the lens ring with the thumb or forefinger of the left hand (taking care never to touch the lens) and then closing down the rest of the fingers so the light is choked off from the lens. To fade in, just reopen the fingers. Most cameras with a manual override have an even better way to achieve fade-in and fade-out. On these cameras set the correct exposure manually, then, while shooting, slowly turn the manual control to the closed-aperture position (the opposite direction from the automatic-exposure position). This causes a gradual dimming of the scene to complete blackness. The procedure can be reversed to achieve fade-in, but be sure to know in advance the correct manual setting to stop at.

Review of Camera Procedure

After the teacher has demonstrated the features of the camera as thoroughly as he feels necessary, the students will be eager to handle the camera. It is probably best to let the students experiment with each aspect of the camera as its function is being discussed. For example, in focusing with a split-level viewfinder a special diagram with vertical and horizontal contrasting lines could be placed across the room. The students could then take turns actually experiencing the camera's focusing.

The following is a check list of the camera's operation. It should be duplicated on a card and included in each camera's carry case with the other shooting equipment. The list could also be used to review the different steps of camera operation with a beginning class before their first shooting.

1. Activate the camera (release run-lock control).
2. Check batteries and camera motors.
3. Load film into the camera and check film counter (and ASA setting, unless Super 8, which is automatic).
4. Remove lens cap (put it in the camera case).
5. Check automatic light exposure meter for adequate light setting. (Make suitable adjustments, such as movie lights.)
6. Choose suitable camera speed.
7. Focus camera and choose appropriate zoom length.
8. Shoot film.

Once again it should be stressed that the teacher need not feel he must be an expert in camera operation in order to teach film making. Excellent films can be made by intelligent use of the instruction manual provided by the camera's manufacturer. Today's camera is so automated that it takes a very short time (less than an hour) for the child to understand its simple technical operation. Students who become enthusiastic about film making will soon outstrip the teacher in technical know-how and will become class leaders and volunteer instructors. As the students develop as film makers and work on progressively more demanding film ideas, help can usually be obtained from the professional film makers and lab technicians in the area.

When the teacher introduces the camera to a beginning class, the information necessary for shooting breaks down easily into categories that approximate the routine of the actual shooting procedure. For example, the teacher will probably first discuss the proper care and maintenance of the camera (as discussed on page 21), just as the film maker would check the batteries and camera condition before loading the camera. Students seem to grasp the camera operation more easily when such a procedure is followed in explaining the camera's technical complexity. The following information is laid out in a pattern approximating the actual shooting routine, but, of course, it would be simplified for presentation to younger classes.

1. Care and maintenance of the camera (pages 20-21).
2. Loading film into the camera (pages 22-25).
3. Handling the camera (pages 26-28).
4. Use of the automatic light meter and its manual override (pages 29-30).
5. Camera speeds and single-frame release (page 31).
6. Focus and the use of the power zoom (pages 32-34).
7. Special effects with the camera (page 34).

What to Shoot

Once they understand and have mastered the simple techniques of shooting, children make wonderful cameramen. More active and mobile than they will be at any time in the rest of their lives, full of imagination and energy, they need little encouragement to capture intriguing material. While all children have the potential to make films as exciting as any of their other art work, their attitude toward the camera is determined to a great extent by the teacher. If the technical demands of film are overemphasized they may "freeze" and work in a much too static way. If they see the camera not in terms of its technicalities but as something to use as freely as a paint brush, their shooting will be spontaneous, ingenious, and appropriate to their age group. Convincing them to think of the camera as an actor who participates in the drama of a film rather than as an observer of a stage presentation who merely records will help to ensure involved, dynamic shooting. On the one hand, children need to be encouraged to shoot from a variety of angles, to move in and out, to get all sorts of information about a subject, to vary quiet passages with lively ones, to keep an eye open for the effect of color against color. On the other hand, they can benefit from suggestions to concentrate their shooting, to develop material related to a definite theme, to avoid random material that will be difficult to edit, and to start shooting with some central idea in mind. As in any art form there are exceptions to every rule. While most children profit from working within a defined theme, some produce beautiful films composed of hundreds of what at first seem to be completely unrelated images. Children working individually develop personal shooting styles, and it is better for the teacher to help them go their own way than to insist they work toward some preconceived goal.

Some teachers may be apprehensive about students shooting at large on their own and perhaps intruding upon the privacy of individuals who do not want to be photo-graphed. But school film-making groups do not seem to run into difficulties in this area. On the whole, people do not seem to mind being photographed by children; evidently they do not present the same threat as an adult with a camera. A child's natural charm plus the telescopic qualities of a zoom lens seem sufficient safeguards against misunderstandings. Insistence upon politeness and a regard for the rights of others is never out of place, of course, but in film making, students must also be encouraged to come to grips with the problem of photographing people as well as things if they are to produce effective films.

Instead of letting each student develop his own projects independently, the group may wish to make its first film a cooperative project — perhaps a film concerned with curriculum content. Such films can be fascinating for even the youngest film-making groups. Not only do they provide motivation for classroom research, but teaching films made by children for children can often be more effective than more sophisticated professional ones. Although they must be concerned with factual accuracy and concentrate on specific subject matter, they must be no less imaginative and attention-getting if they are to achieve their purpose. Lively editing and inventive camerawork are necessary ingredients of every curriculum film, but they must be closely coordinated so that educational points can be made clearly and concisely. Because of this, a shooting script will be much more necessary than in most school films. Such a script might be no more than a data list of information that needs to be gathered, or it could outline a shooting sequence consisting of related episodes. Script material for such films should be based on research appropriate to the age level concerned. Its organization will be fresher and more appealing if it grows out of group discussions and group decisions.

Camerawork which involves the viewer optically by the use of a variety of shooting angles and by interspersing medium shots with close-ups and long shots not only keeps his interest but helps to orient him to the film's purposes. Here we see students making a film on marine zoology as they discuss the script and make a sequence of shots.

Then the camera is placed on the tripod and our eye is led to the subject matter by a medium shot . . .

. . . and then a close-up.

As the script calls for a progressively detailed study, the cameraman slowly zooms in to a medium closeup that shows the symmetrical configuration of the starfish and then to an extreme closeup that reveals its surface structure. When a film calls for the camera to move in to less than four or five feet from an object the image on the viewing glass must be closely scrutinized with the zoom fully extended to ascertain whether a clear image can be obtained at that range. If the definition is at all uncertain, it pays to shift the camera back until there is no doubt it is in sharp focus. Some cameras can move in much closer than this, and all cameras can be fitted with close-up attachments to facilitate such shooting.

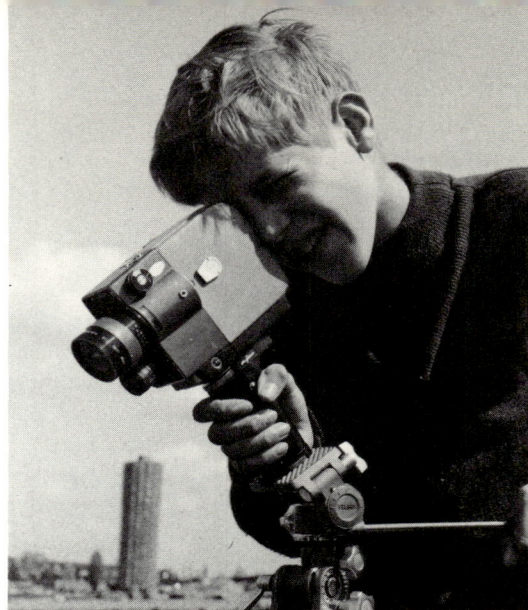

43

PROJECTORS

A good projector is, after the camera, the most important piece of equipment for school film making. Formerly a film teacher would try to teach one or two mechanically inclined youngsters to act as projectionists for the whole class. But the 8mm and Super 8 projectors have become so easy to use that every student, after brief instruction, can and should learn how to run one for himself. The beginner will use the machine only as a tool to view his first rushes, but as he develops his skills, the creative and interpretative potentiality of the projector in film presentations will become more evident.

Most modern machines are self-threading. That is, if the leader film is in good condition and properly trimmed (different types of projectors usually have different kinds of trimmers built into their chassis), it is placed into an aperture and the film proceeds to thread itself through the sprockets to the take-up reel. Occasionally the projector will fail to carry the film all the way through. This is usually because the leader is damaged or creased. The best remedy is to cut off the damaged or worn leader and start again. It may be necessary to splice on new leader, so a spare supply of leader film and a splicer should be part of the projectionist's equipment. Older 8mm projectors were hand-fed, like the 16mm machines that most teachers have used. Film loops are required at the top and bottom of the lens, which hinges out to permit the film to be inserted into a track passing over the light aperture. As there is seldom sound in these machine, the threading is actually simpler than the 16mm and little can go wrong.

The trend in projectors is toward cartridge or cassette feeding, just as it has been in camera and tape recorders. This system is especially convenient for young children, but it will undoubtedly prove attractive to older classroom film makers as well. At present, or at least until the new Kodak cartridge system becomes widely marketed, it is still an inconvenience to install the student's film in cassettes, and the cartridge projectors are not generally as flexible as the better self-threading ones.

If the cameras the students are using are a mixture of 8mm and Super 8 or the film club has a collection of 8mm films, then a dual-8 projector (one that converts from 8mm to Super 8) is the best choice. If the projector is flexible enough it can be used for editing as well as contributing greatly to the enjoyment and creative showing of the completed film. Most projectors have a reverse control that will run the film backwards and a "still" control that will stop the film on a single frame. (If the camera doesn't have a still control the film should never be stopped with the lamp still on, or the heat of the lamp will burn the film. When a still control is operated, a protective transparent lens moves in front of the film to shield it from the lamp.) The student is able to study his film more thoroughly before editing by using the projector's reverse controls to rerun a special section until he decides where to cut the film. He can stop the film, using the still control, on the right image and mark the film near the intended cut with a china-marking pencil.

Better projectors such as the Kodak Instamatic "M 80-90" series and some new Bell and Howell "Autoloads" feature a selection of speeds forward and reverse that enables the student to exhibit their films in slow and fast motion as well as the normal speed. The Kodak, for example, has speeds of 6 and 54 frames per second as well as the standard 18. This may at first appear to be somewhat of a frill, useful mainly for comic effect. But students soon find that they can script into their films slow and quick passages that greatly heighten the effectiveness. A few projectors are equipped with zoom lenses, which, if they are of sufficient quality, add yet another opportunity to refine an already completed film. Some students become so adept at using all the capacities of the projector that, synchronized with sound from tape or record, the film showing itself becomes an exciting personal performance.

It is worth budgeting for a fairly expensive projector (around $150 to $200), as it will be in constant and sometimes arduous use. An efficient, strong, and flexible projector will contribute a great deal toward a mechanically smooth operation. As different projectors tend to run at slightly different speeds the student naturally wishes to show his film on the projector he used when he synchronized the sound tape. The projector should, therefore, be relatively portable, since the students may wish to show films in many different circumstances.

Some of the most expensive projectors have built-in recording and sound-amplifying equipment. Its advantages and disadvantages are discussed on pages 72-75.

Although older 8mm projectors are hand-fed, little can go wrong with threading.

ORGANIZATION AND SUPERVISION

Storage and Loan of Equipment

Although the basic concerns of school film making are creativity and aesthetics, the day-by-day problems are more likely to be practical than esoteric. Unless there is a proper organization, the tasks of distributing, collecting, and keeping track of equipment, tapes, and films can easily become inordinately time-consuming. Unfortunately, the more successful a program, the more pressing its practical problems become.

If this side of film making is well organized from the beginning and a logical and easy-to-understand system of distribution and collection is instituted early, time spent in checking equipment in and out can be cut to a minimum and much confusion will be avoided. No matter how well designed such a system is, however, its effectiveness will never be realized unless its rules are strictly followed.

As each piece of equipment is acquired it should be labeled, catalogued, given an appropriate container, and assigned a storage area. Here we see how the Middle School Film Club at the Collegiate School in New York City organizes its materials and equipment. Every camera has a case with a shoulder strap; record players, projectors, and editors are in cases with handles; splicers, splices, extra bulbs, and so on are stored in cigar boxes. Everything is labeled and numbered, and everything has a storage space to which it must be returned. Equipment that might be used out of school has the school address attached. Films and tapes that have been edited are stored in numbered racks for screening. Extension cords and spare reels are hung where they are easily visible, and after one is used it is always returned to the same place.

So that whoever borrows a camera can be sure he has a complete set of equipment and can use it correctly, each camera case should have a supplies and equipment check-off list included in it, along with a camera procedure check list (see page 35).

The check-off list should include the following:

1. Manual (or set of instructions if camera manual is not available).
2. Spare batteries — a complete set for camera motors. (A spare mercury battery need not be included, as these last up to two years. Regular replacement is suggested.)
3. Lens cap.
4. Dust cover or plug for Type A filter slot.
5. Key for Type A filter slot.
6. Rubber eye cap (in some cases).
7. Filters, adapters.
8. Lens tissues (for older students.)
9. Blower brush (for cleaning lens).
10. Detachable pistol grip (for some cameras).
11. Tripod (optional).
12. Movie light and bracket (optional).
13. Release cable (optional).
14. Lens shade (optional).

This list should be checked when the camera is taken out and again when it is brought back. When items are missing, their replacement should not be postponed; missing parts should be tracked down immediately.

Students are more likely to respond with enthusiasm to an organizational arrangement when they are involved in setting it up. Playing an active part in planning a system of checking equipment in and out and then themselves doing the labeling and cataloguing not only insures that they will want to see their efforts put to good use but guarantees that they will understand the system.

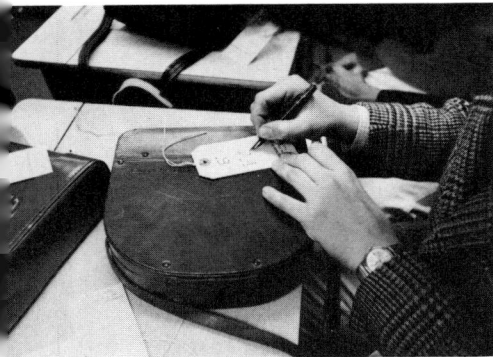

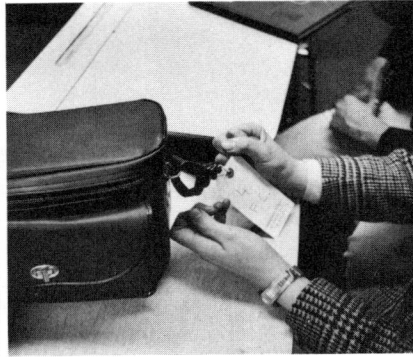

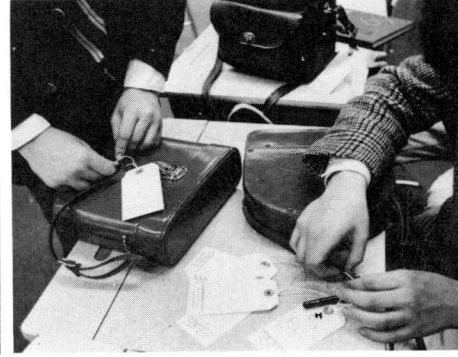

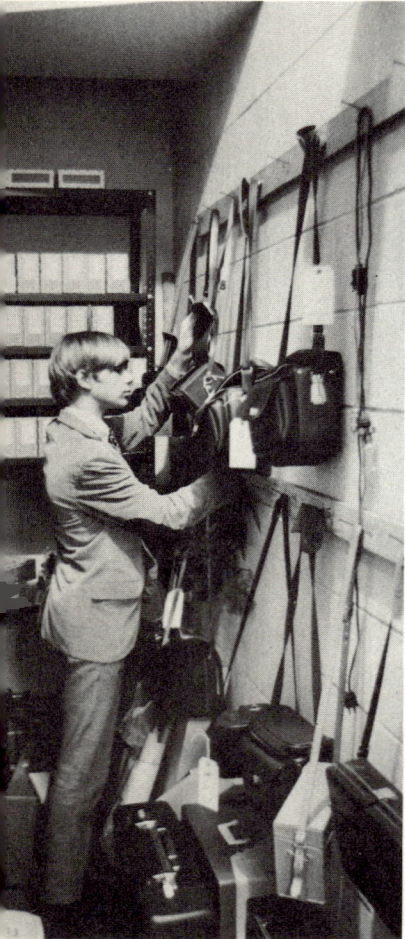

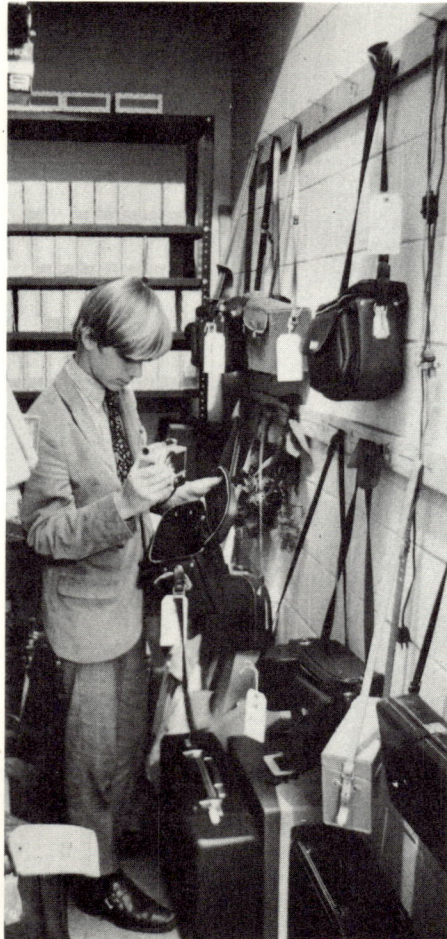

While students should be allowed a maximum of freedom from rules in creating their films, rules for borrowing equipment and materials must be strict. All arrangements should be simple and regulations crystal-clear. For example, it might be a good idea to decide that cameras can be taken out only on Monday afternoons from 3:30 to 4:30 p.m., kept for only one week, and returned only on Monday mornings from 8:15 to 8:45 a.m., this also being the only time that film is accepted for processing. Such a schedule will confine bookkeeping to one day a week and, if no exceptions are made, will set a pattern of taking out and returning cameras that students will accept and abide by. Distributing equipment at random upsets any kind of

regularized procedure and makes keeping track a hit-and-miss affair.

Each camera, editor, and other article should be logged out carefully and then logged in on hectographed or mimeographed forms designed to make spotting missing items and tracking them down comparatively simple. When established procedures are regularized and forms are easy to understand and fill out, there is no reason why students should not take on this type of responsibility. Hours for lending and returning equipment should be quite separate from those set aside for instruction or the viewing and discussion of rushes, so that the real business of film making will not be interrupted by routine. Records of equipment logged in and out should be kept on file even when everything has been returned, as even a brief glance over a term's entries will indicate which cameras and editors are popular and which ones students avoid. This will give some direction for future purchases. It is a temptation to keep good camera equipment out of circulation, and it is a mistake to do so. Children, on the whole, treat cameras with respect, and they do such fine work on their own that it is well worth giving them every opportunity to exercise their unusual film-making facility — even when it means allowing an eleven-year-old to go off by himself with an expensive camera, or trusting a nine-year-old with a cherished editor.

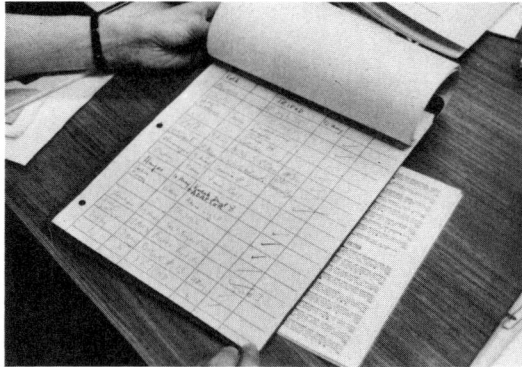

is shown reel by reel. At the conclusion of each reel, the film maker — or film makers, if more than one student is involved — can indicate what footage might be removed because of technical flaws and listen to general suggestions along this line. When all the reels have been screened, the suggested construction of the whole film, along with the editing of individual sections, can be analyzed.

Whatever aspect of the film is being considered, the film maker's ideas about how he wants to handle it must always be respected, but he should be encouraged to listen to suggestions and to discuss his ideas fully with the group.

The teacher should function as a group leader and as a vocal member of the group. Much of his direction can take the form of suggestions made in much the same spirit as any other member of the class. From time to time he can contribute technical information, and he may well act as an informal chairman, especially when a number of films have to be shown in a limited time. Although the teacher's opinions in such sessions will influence to a great extent the sensitivity and inventiveness of the films produced and their integrity as personal statements, it is important that his suggestions be extremely oblique so that the young film maker never loses confidence in himself and can enjoy the satisfaction of feeling he has produced a film that is really his own.

When a film-making program first gets under way, such group sessions will probably be concerned with discussing rushes that the whole group has produced. When such a program is well established, however, some film makers will begin to bring in films that they have shot and edited completely on their own. If they are used to having their material discussed, they will welcome having their films screened by the group and will look forward to participating in a critique.

Working with Unedited Film

While most youngsters are keen to make a film that is in every way their own, they need and want the support and confidence that comes from sharing both their enthusiasms and and their problems with a group. This group experience is richest when the members of a class or club sit down together to watch developed but unedited films projected for the first time.

In such a viewing session a suggested procedure is to have a student film maker who has some unedited film to show tell how he plans to organize his material. If he is basing it on a poem he has written, he might read it; if he has done a study of a neighborhood, he could tell something about the conditions there; and so on. Then the film

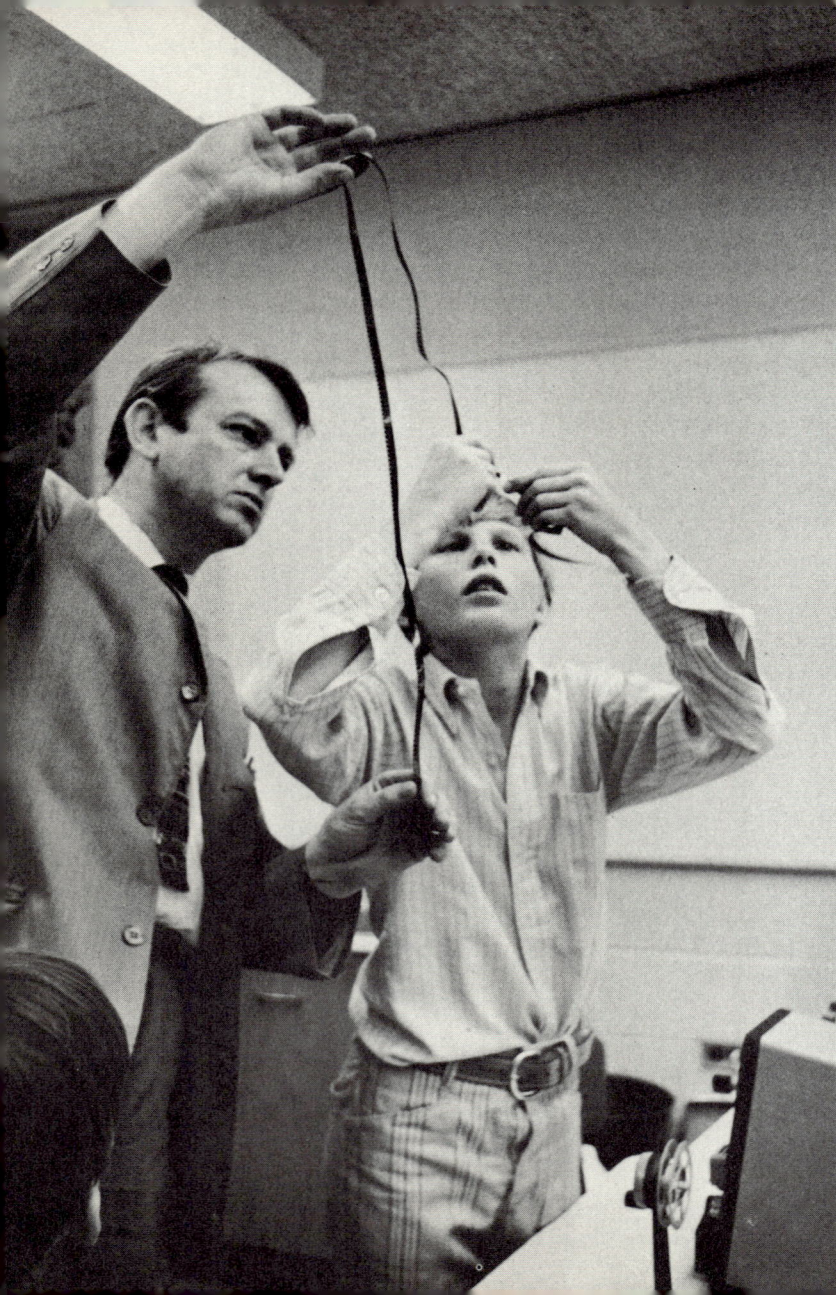

EDITING

Once the film maker has had his footage processed he is ready to organize it into some sort of film order that best meets his purpose.

Uncomplicated films can be "edited" in the camera. That is, actual shooting can be so organized that one episode follows another in some sort of understandable and aesthetically acceptable sequence. Such films can be shown as is or with only the evidences of poor camerawork removed. Some very successful school films have been made in this way, and a camera-edited film is a fine prelude to more complicated film making.

In most cases, however, the film maker will have to go to greater lengths to produce a finished film. First, he must examine his processed film, cutting out sections marred by light flashes, overexposure and underexposure, evidences of too fast panning, faulty focusing, and so on. Then, he must set about establishing a cinematic scheme that tells a story, creates a mood, or expresses an idea in the way he feels will be most effective. Sometimes he may even decide that he must shoot more footage if he is to achieve what he has in mind. Children will very often re-edit their films in several different ways, and their attitude toward their work changes as they gain new insights into film making.

Every step in making a film contributes toward its final form, but editing, to a very great extent, establishes its character. Today's youngster, having spent many hours viewing TV and movies, is aware of manipulation of time and understands what editing will do to the material that has been filmed. Just as he should be encouraged to explore his subject creatively with the camera, he should be urged to be bold and innovative when editing.

Editing, particularly if there is a great deal of cutting and splicing to do, can be a time-consuming and arduous job. Every effort should be made to keep it from becoming a chore. Some procedures, routine in the laboratory, are too demanding for the classroom and are best replaced by simpler steps that may not always assure clean film and splices but are more likely to result in lively and interesting films. Editing procedures that are not complex prepare students to work on their own at home or in free time at school, while more complicated procedures tend to over-formalize editing and take up class time.

Children need a good deal of help with editing. While such assistance in school film making will have to be organized by the teacher, the less direct and more oblique it can be, the better. Students' satisfaction in film making comes from accomplishments that are uniquely their own and that express their ideas. The teacher's efforts should be so directed that the group or the individual can experience such satisfaction.

Perhaps the best technique is to work through the group. Every school film maker is jealous of each foot of film he has shot and is often blind to any imperfections that are in it. Effective editing has to begin with a critical examination of everything that has been shot. Technically flawed footage can be spotted on the film or in the editor, but irrelevant or uninspired material shows up best when projected. It does not take students long to know what will not project well technically, and they have little hesitation in discarding such footage. Material that is good optically but doubtful in other regards is another problem. Here is where the group approach is effective. When the class looks at material it has shot collectively, or when several

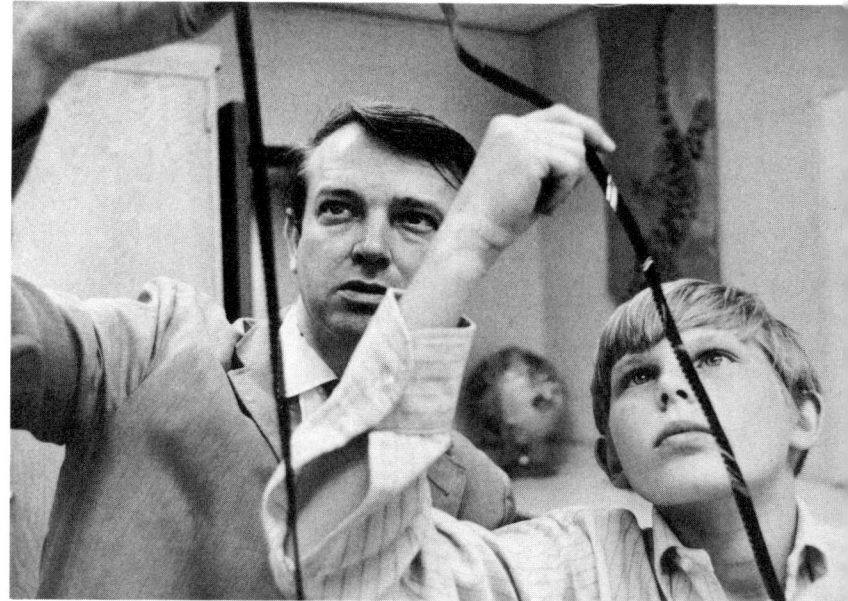

individuals show footage that they have shot and explain how they will use it, the reaction of the group gives a foretaste of how audiences in general will react to the same material in the finished film. Suggestions as to what might be deleted, added, or shortened, particularly if there is a difference of opinion, give the beginning film maker a direction for his editing that is helpful but does not interfere with his own artistic decision-making. At the same time, his own participation in such group appraisals helps to make him progressively more and more aware of what is cinematically effective and what is not. Older children should be encouraged to jot down suggestions at such screenings, particularly when they concern technical details and timing. Films that evolve organically out of the child's own ideas and that are helped to conclusion by the suggestions of other children have a better chance of retaining the freshness of young ideas than those that are only childish interpretations of adult ideas.

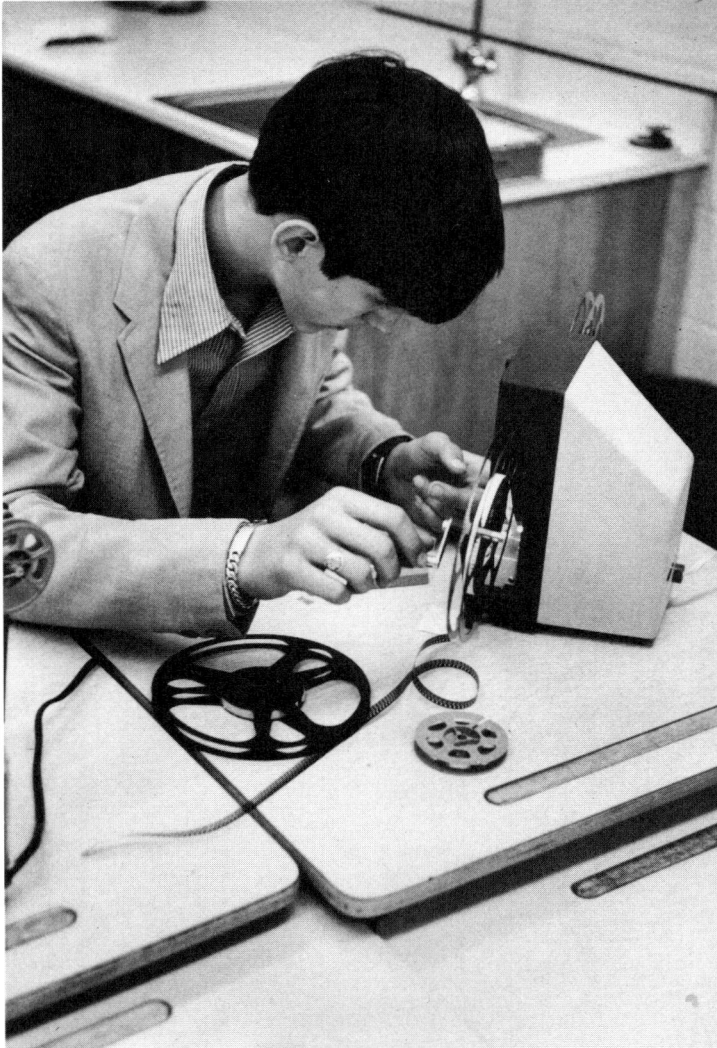

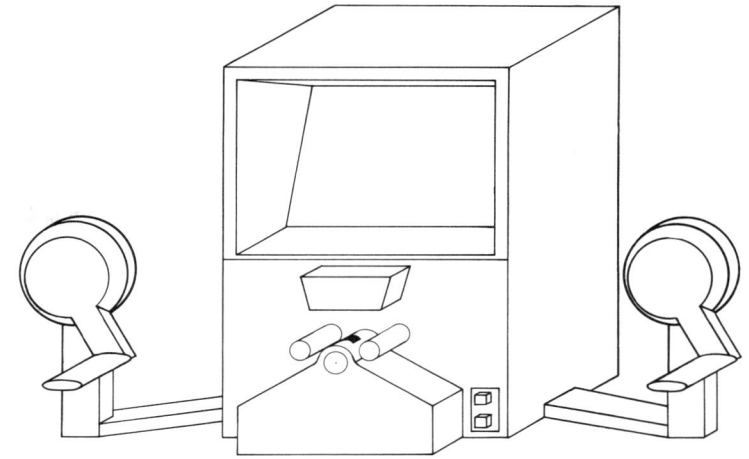

Editors and Splicers

Just as a wise choice of a camera will facilitate shooting, so will the right type of editor for the classroom make editing easier. An editor for school use should be sturdier than one that might be satisfactory for home use. It is advisable to get one that will handle both 8mm and Super 8 film. If possible it is best to buy half a dozen spare bulbs when purchasing an editor and several 100-foot reels, both 8mm and Super 8. Reels should be chosen with some care. Metal reels with a slot into which the end of the film can be inserted are best for children. In equipping a classroom it is a good idea to match each camera with an editor and a splicer. Some editors come equipped with a splicer attached; this is not as convenient an arrangement as it may seem, because it ties the splicer down when it might be used to advantage by one student when another is using the editor only for preliminary cutting. Splicers are not expensive and the group should have as many as they are apt to need at any one time.

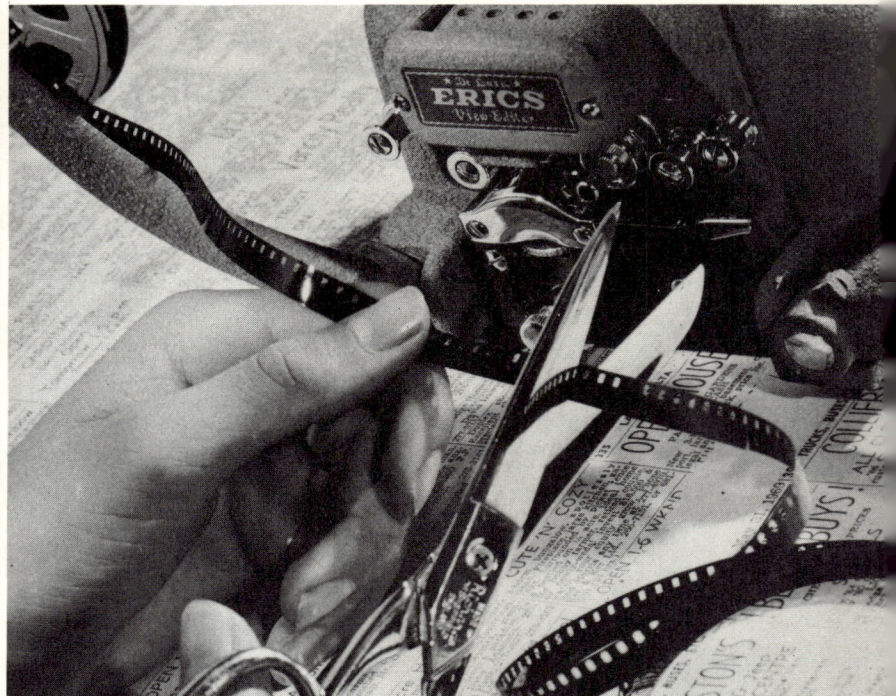

A Simple Editing Project

Once he has had a chance to view all his processed film, the film maker runs it through an editor, using a pair of scissors both to remove spoiled lengths and to separate subject areas. He cuts the film where one area butts up against the next. Many editors have an indicator blade which, when depressed, nicks or perforates the edge of the film when the appropriate frame appears on the viewing glass. Film can also be marked with a china-marking pencil at the film gate to indicate where it should be cut. The division point between adjoining sequences is usually easily visible when film is help up to the light, and many children prefer doing the preliminary cutting of their film completely by eye. In the laboratory, a technician would always wear lint-free white gloves when handling film. In the classroom this is not practical, but the film should always be held by its edges, and lengths of film must rest on a clean surface. Film that is edited out should never be discarded but stored, as it might be useful in the future. Technically flawed film can be used by beginners in learning how to splice and, if regular leader is not available, as emergency leader.

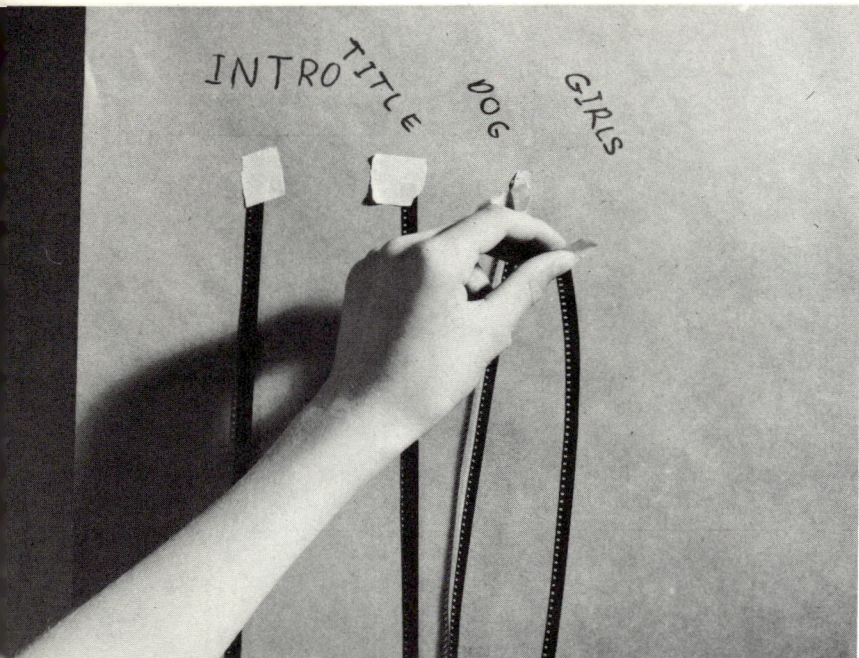

As the film maker runs through his footage, cutting out lengths that are concerned with a common topic, he must work out some system to organize his work and to keep it clean. Here the film maker has used masking tape to fasten a sheet of Kraft paper to the wall. To this he tapes lengths of film, labeling each one. The tapes fall free on a clear surface in a way that keeps them from tangling and makes them easy to identify.

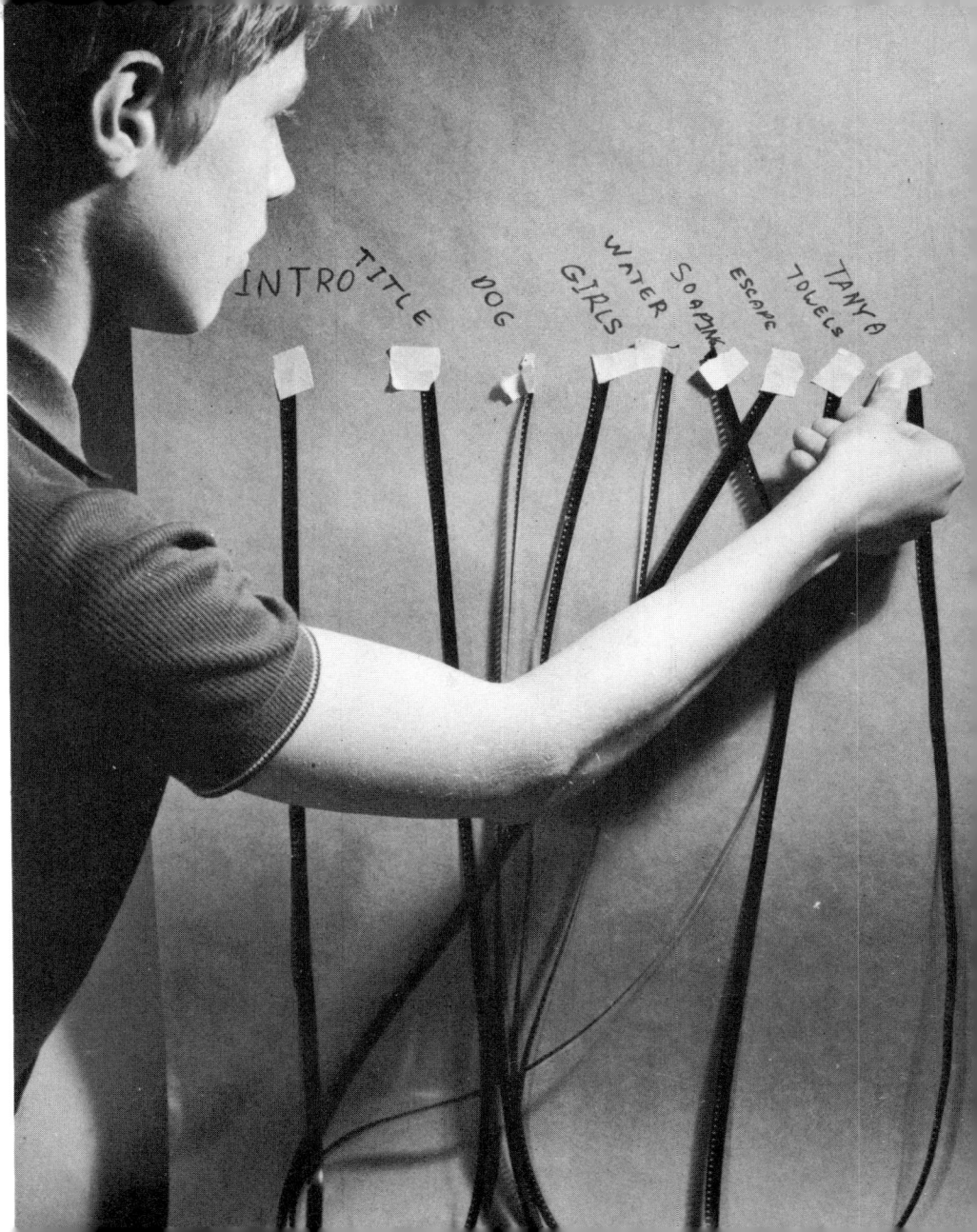

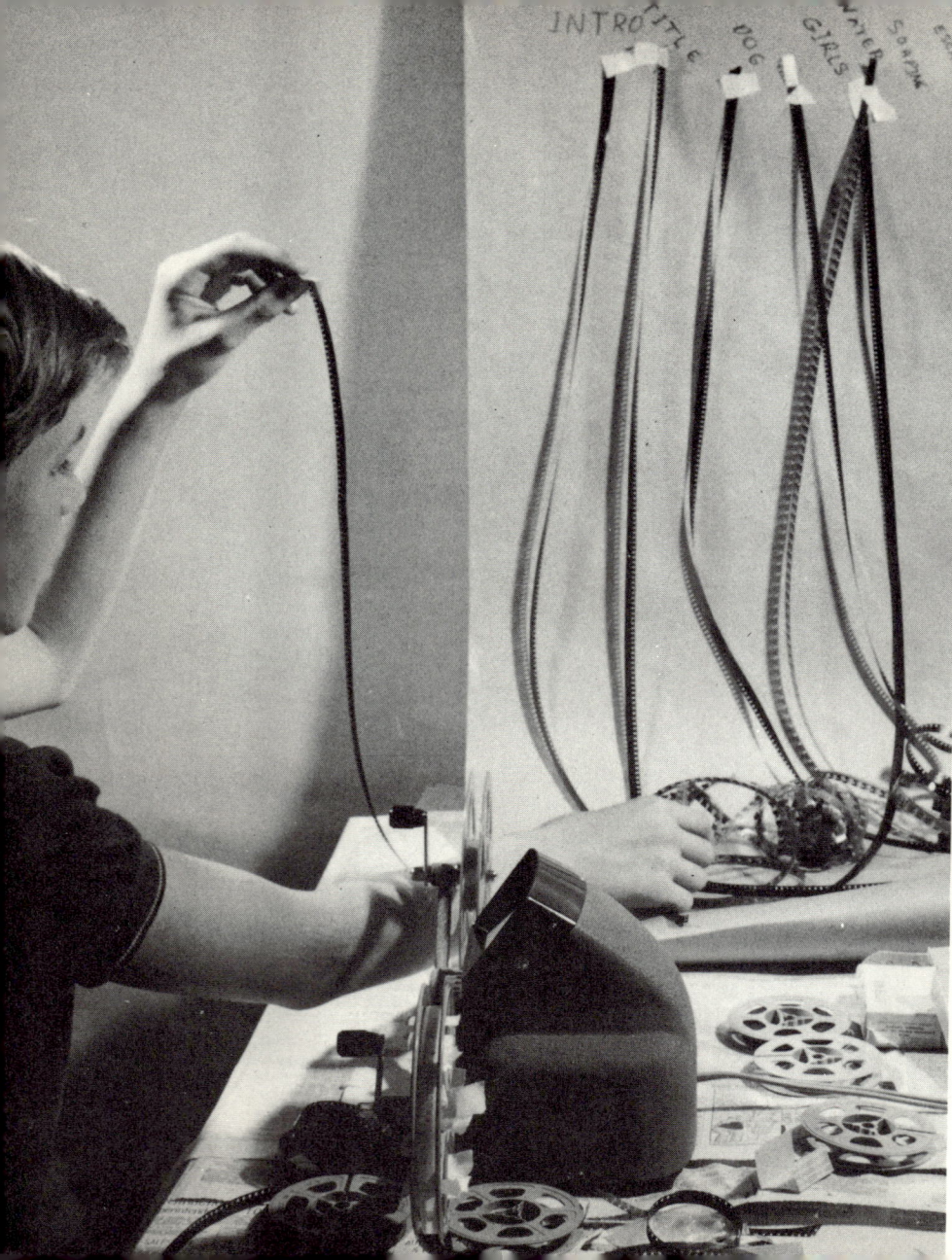

1

2

Once all the parts of the film are organized in labeled lengths, the order in which these are to appear on the screen can be established. Here the film maker takes one length at a time (1) and, beginning with the opening sequence, uses masking tape to fasten one length to the next (2), then winds each taped section onto the right-hand reel of the editor (3). As he winds each length onto the reel he inserts a paper tab to indicate where it begins. This is not always necessary, but if there is to be much cross-cutting (one length is cut up and its parts inserted between other sequences), it helps to speed up editing. Eventually every length is taped into place and some sort of order is established. At this point, the fim maker may decide to shorten some sequences and cross-cut others, and, as the masking tape is easily removed, he can wind his film back and forth, taking out pieces here and there and interspersing others along its whole length. Finally, a continuity is established, the taped film is wound back on the left-hand reel (4) so that the opening scene is at the beginning, paper tabs are removed, and the film is ready for splicing.

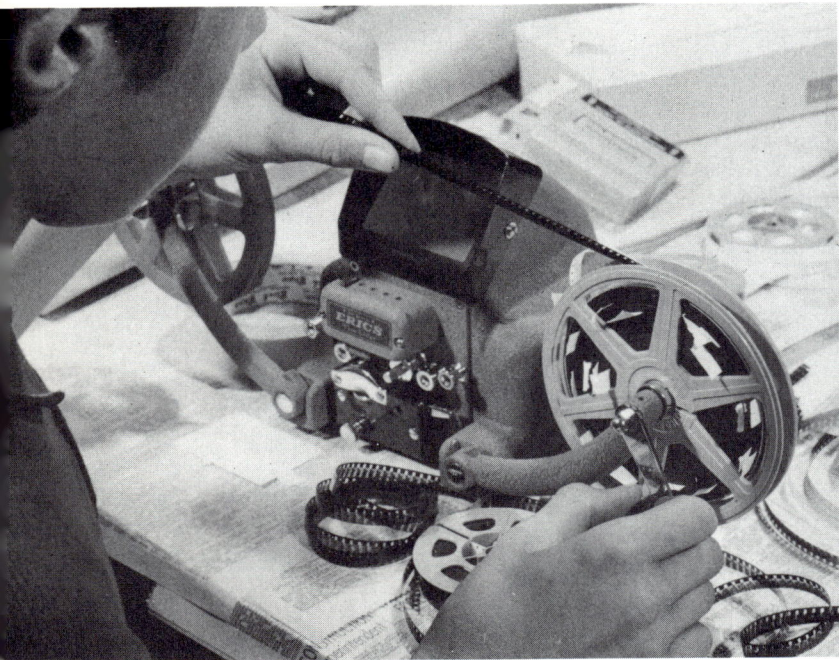

3

4

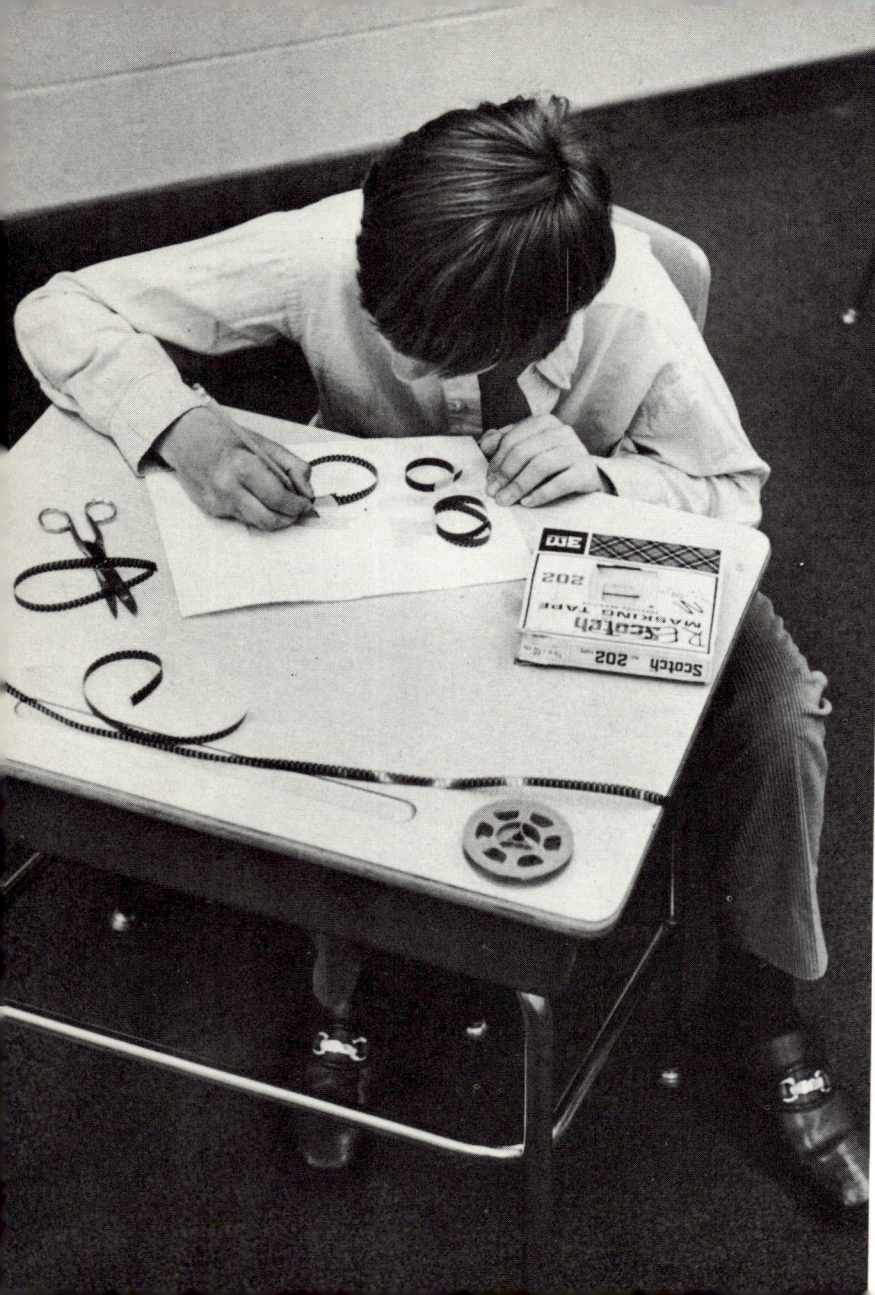

Some Suggestions for Classroom Editing

When a school film-making program gets into full swing, editing can become a bottleneck that interferes with the completion of films and causes delays that can easily dampen enthusiasm. It is better to adapt editing to the classroom situation than to insist on orthodox procedures that are difficult to follow. Here are two methods of organizing film that lend themselves to individual film making in the classroom and are handy when film is to be taken home for editing. In one, coils of film are placed in the depressions of an egg carton and numbered. Corresponding numbers and descriptions of sequences are listed on an accompanying sheet of paper. In the other, lengths of film are coiled into small loops and fastened by tabs of masking tape to a sheet of cardboard or heavy paper and labeled by writing on the backing sheet.

Splicing

When the film is just the way the film maker wants it and, if necessary, a title and ending have been added, it is ready to be spliced. In splicing, each masking-tape tab is replaced by either a wet or dry splice, which will firmly adhere one length of film to the next without interfering with projection. As previously suggested, it is wise not to throw away pieces of film discarded in editing but to use them for beginners to practice splicing. Good splices should be as sturdy as whole film yet so effectively match one section of film to the next as to be invisible when the film is projected. Splicing is a highly individualized skill, so that after a film program has been in progress for some time it is best to have experienced students help beginners to learn.

Dry splicing is the most practical technique for the classroom. It is quite easy to learn. Good prints can be made from film that is dry-spliced, and dry splices stand up as well even when a film is shown over and over again. Wet splicing is a more complicated technique and is more suited to individual film making. Some film makers contend that wet splices make a "neater" film, and students who have made several films will want to try it. In organizing classroom film making, however, it is best to emphasize dry techniques.

Dry Splicing

Dry splicing is an easily mastered step-by-step skill. With a little perseverance and quite a lot of practice the students become very adept. Some editors come with a splicer built in, while other editors include a separate splicer in the package. Most students seem to prefer the larger and more heavily constructed separate splicer. The Kodak splicer shown below can splice Super 8 film as well as 8mm and 16mm. Note the double row of sprocket pins. The splicer used in the step-by-step photographs splices only 8mm and 16mm. The dual-8 splicer is a better purchase for most film classes. The different makes of splicers are all reasonable in cost, and the students should experiment to see what kind they prefer.

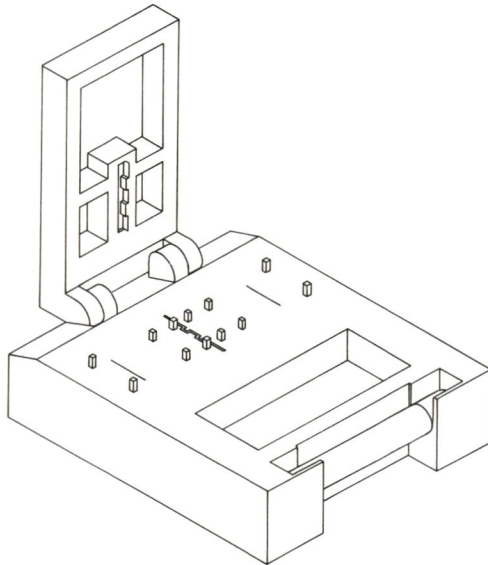

1. Lift the cutting-knife handle. Place one of the film strips, emulsion or dull side down, on the splicer base so that the film sprocket holes are pressed down over the two fixed pins and the movable pin on the left-hand side. The end of the film should extend over the cutting line.

2. *Place the other film strip, emulsion side down also, over the three pins on the right side of the splicer base. The end of this film must extend over the center line to the left side, so that the strips overlap.*

3. *Press down the cutting handle firmly to cut through the double layer of film. (When the cutting blade becomes dull a new one can be purchased from the local dealer or from the maker.)*

4. *After raising the cutting-knife handle, carefully remove the top trimmed end of film without disturbing the two film strips.*

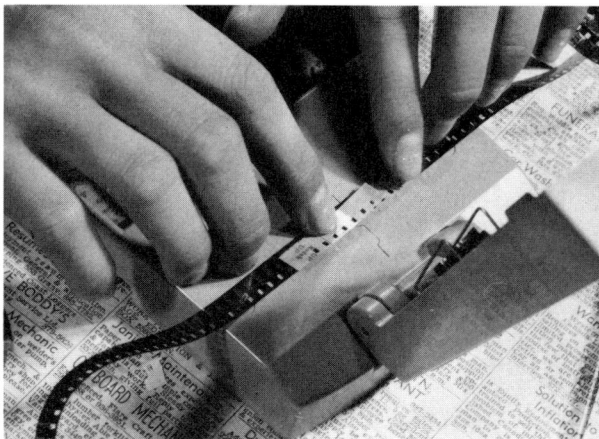

5. *Place a splicing tape or "press tape" printed side up on the four fixed pins over the butted film ends. The center line of the tape will be over the cut line and the cut ends of the film.*

6. *This is the tricky step. It is rather like applying a Band-Aid to a cut. Hold one side of the tape down, and carefully . . .*

7. *. . . pull off the opposite side's paper flap. Press the tape down to seal it to the film, taking care that the sprocket perforations of the tape and the film coincide.*

8. Now, hold the taped side firmly down, gently pull off the other paper flap, and . . .

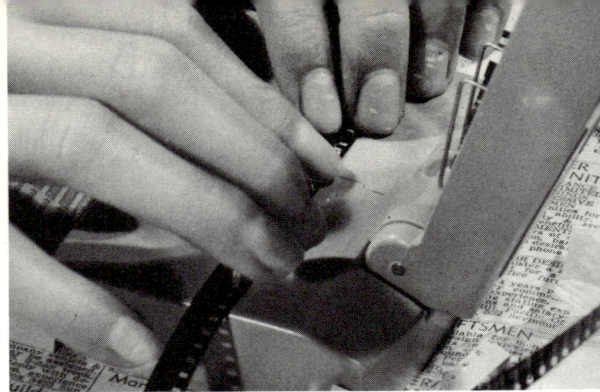

9. . . . rub the tape down to get a good contact, again paying attention to the sprocket perforations. Some splicers have special rubbing tools, but a fingernail usually does just as well.

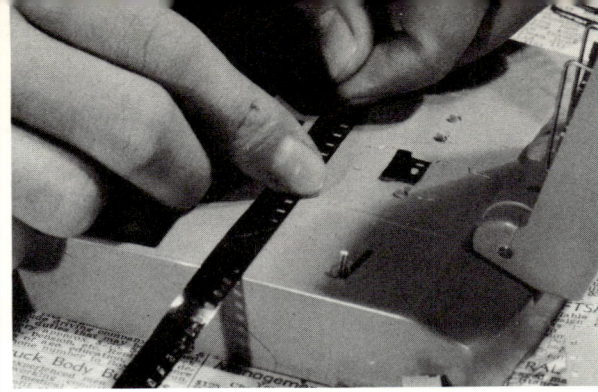

10. Remove the film from the pins and discard the remaining trimmed edge. Place the film on the splicer base and, using the back of a fingernail (notice left forefinger), rub down the splice until it is transparent and smooth.

11. Turn the film over (emulsion side up) and place on splicer pins. Sprocket holes are now on the bottom of the film.

12. Apply the press tape in the same manner as before (in steps 5, 6, 7, 8, and 9). The film join is now sandwiched between two press tapes.

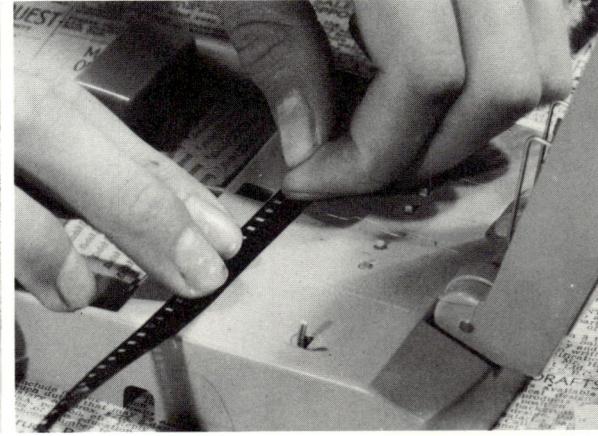

13. Rub down smoothly with fingernail. Make sure that the sprocket holes are left clear and that the joint is butted cleanly with no overlap or space visible.

Wet Splicing

1. Check to be sure two strips of film are both emulsion (dull) side up.

2. Fit one strip to the guide pins.

67

3. Bring down upper plate to secure, then raise the whole unit on that side up.

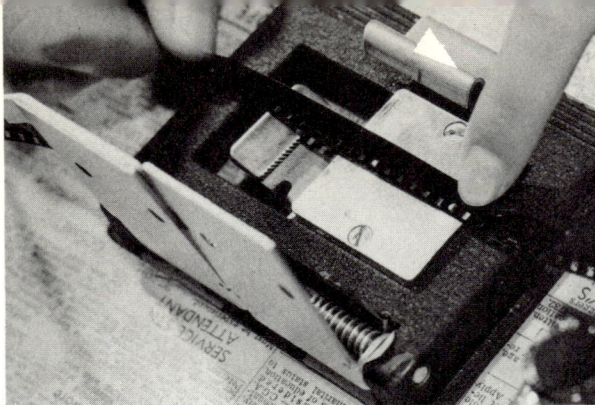

4. Position other strip on guide pins. Note built-in scraper below film: on some splicers the scraper is separate.

5. The plate is brought down to hold film firmly in position.

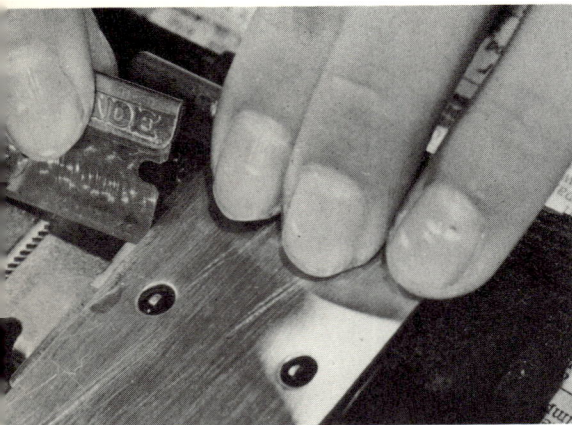

9. In this case the scraper did not do a thorough job, so a razor blade is used to make the film base absolutely clean. Otherwise the film cement cannot adhere properly.

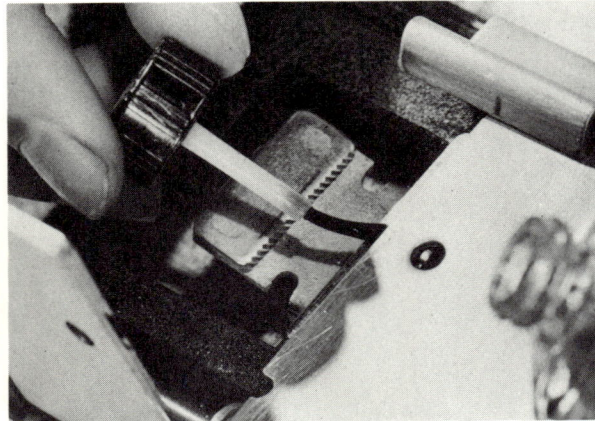

10. Film cement is applied to the film edge. Be sure the film cement is fresh; stale cement is one of the main causes of failure. Keep the cement tightly corked at all times.

11. Immediately after the cement is applied, the other side, the pressure plate, is brought down. In this particular splicer this releases the other retaining side so it springs up; not all splicers have this feature.

6. Bring the first unit down. Its edge will snip through the second film strip.

7. As the first unit is raised up again, the small edge of the cut-off film can be seen.

8. The scraper is moved back and forth to take the emulsion off. The disadvantage of built-in scrapers is that they can become dull and cannot be replaced.

12. The raised plate permits any excess cement to be wiped off the film so it will not soften the other part. Under the pressure plate the film cement fuses the two strips together.

13. After fifteen or twenty seconds the other plate can be raised and the splice should be complete.

14. Pull the film off the pins gently, as the splice may not be fully set. The splice will harden in a few seconds and will be as strong and permanent as the film itself.

Different Approaches to Editing

A good film must have more than just good editing or good camerawork or good sound. It must be a composite of these set into a structure that allows one to complement the other. Films can be worlds apart in subject matter and treatment but still be equally effective if these three elements support one another.

Here are excerpts from two 8mm films that differ sharply in camerawork, editing, sound, and concept, although they were made by students belonging to the same film club.

The first sequence of frames is from a film made out of school by an eighth-grade student. The film consists basically of a series of vaguely related images shot in color and arranged in chance order. A continuity of sorts is established by another series of short black-and-white newsreel-type sequences (from a commercially produced 8mm film), which are interspersed between the color sequences throughout the film.

In evolving his film the student did not attempt to establish a story line or deliver any type of message. Its design is completely open-ended, and there is no particular relationship between one part of the film and another. He accentuated its random quality by coloring over some sequences with magic markers, deliberately scratching through the color on some of these, throwing some sequences out of focus, working with abstraction here, reality there, coloring in some individual frames and overlaying others with a design or texture. The camerawork, on the whole, in fairly straightforward, and there are few attempts at varying the camera angle. In keeping with the film's abstract quality, he chose an electronic sound track devoid of melody and full of dissonance but with a persistent, pulsing beat that matched the alternation of color and black-and-white sequences.

The second film was made not by an individual student, but by a group of sixth- and seventh-grade children. It is organized in an easily comprehended, logical manner. One scene follows the next in almost predictable order. In this particular sequence, a school cameraman is chased by an angry umbrella-wielding victim of his candid photography.

In contrast to the first film, none of the footage has been colored or scratched or thrown out of focus. Close-ups, middle distance shots, and long shots have been used to give visual variety. Three students shot this sequence; from up close, from the fire escape of a nearby building, and from a moving station wagon. Cameramen (with empty cameras) and actors rehearsed the scene several times before it was filmed.

Music with a strongly defined melody and, at some points, lyrics that match the action provide, in contrast to the first film, a conservative but appropriate sound track.

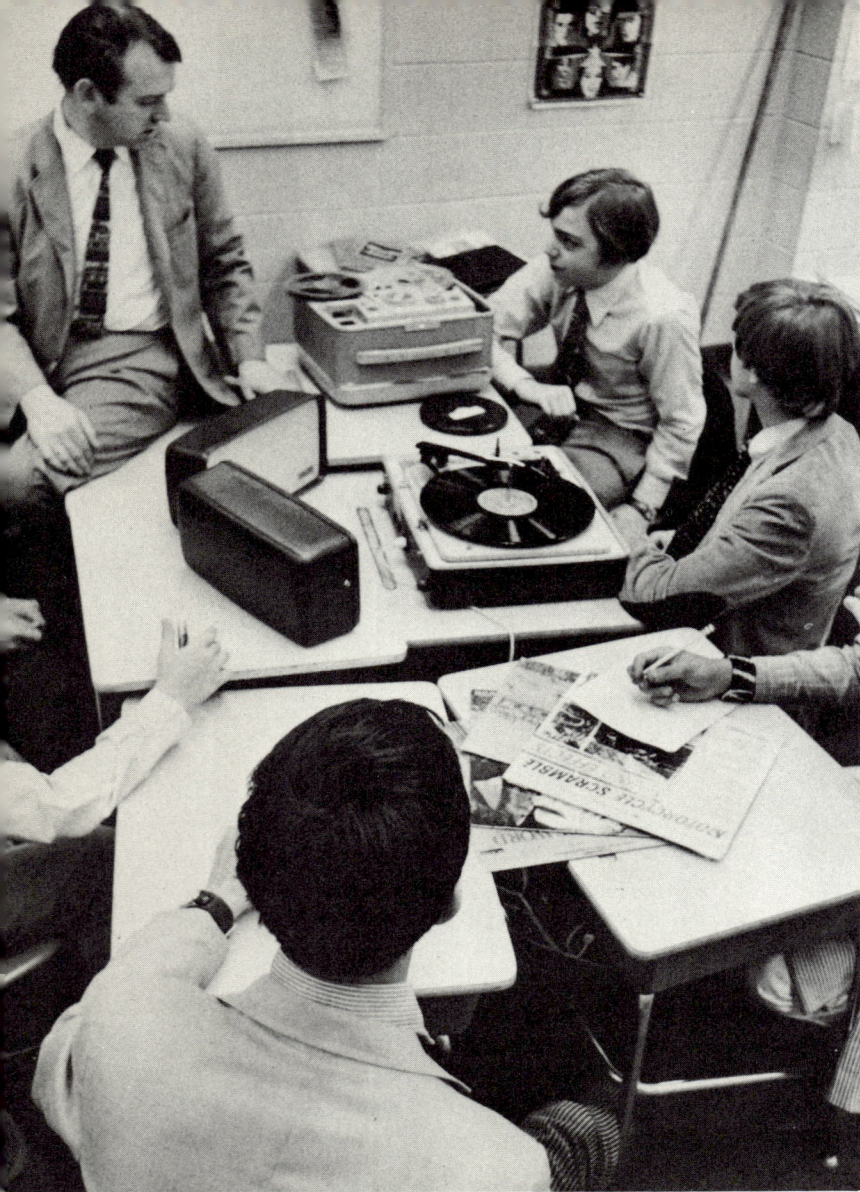

SOUND

Sound is integral to film, not merely an enhancement. Some films, in fact, find their inspiration in sound and are built around sound. Film images can integrate sound as easily as sound can reinforce imagery, and there is no reason why film cannot help to structure auditory experience in the same way as sound helps to define visual experience.

Sound in film can mean music, conversation, noise, even silence. Whether it is synchronized to speech and movement on the screen or is used less specifically, it goes a long way to establish a film's effectiveness. Some children become so intrigued with the possibilities of sound that it can become their major film interest, especially if sound is explored in creative ways.

Appropriate sound equipment is as important to film making as is appropriate camera equipment. A good record player along with both a standard and a portable tape recorder will be an effective basic sound unit, although a school group can do interesting work with just a tape recorder or just a record player. Whenever possible it is best to record music by a direct hook-up between record player and tape recorder in order to avoid random sounds.

Sound can be added to film in one of three ways. Perhaps the best way for the classroom is by the production of an accompanying tape. After a film has been edited and spliced it can be projected and the sound taped to match the sequence of images on the screen. If any recording is done with an open microphone, caution must be taken to avoid picking up the noise of the projector. The projector can be positioned outside a classroom and project through the glass of the closed door. Both the projector and the tape recorder can be stopped when necessary. The tape

can be erased and sound re-recorded at will, so that it is not too difficult to match sound to image. Good sound reproduction will come from running the tape at $7^1/_2$ inches per second. While there should be little difficulty making sound conform generally to film action, accurate synchronization of sound to movement or to speech is too complex an operation for this method, though some synchronization is possible. A crayon mark on the tape where the sound starts and another on the film where the sound should commence will help cordinate sound and action. Place the crayon mark on the tape in the sound head of the recorder (which has been warmed up); when the mark on the film appears on the screen, turn on the recorder.

It is well to remember that tape recorders and projectors run at different speeds. It is wise, in running a film, to use the original equipment on which the sound was recorded and the film initially projected. When the sound seems just right the crayon mark on the film should be replaced with ink or a scratch, and a short length of colored leader tape can be spliced to the recording tape to indicate where the sound starts.

The second way to record sound is directly in the projector. Before this method can be used, however, a laboratory print of the original spliced and edited film must be made with a sound strip bonded along its edge. When this has been done, sound can be added in the same way as has been outlined above. Recording in the projector, of course, makes accurate synchronization much more feasible, but as the sound amplification in 8mm and Super 8 projectors is limited, reproduction suffers. A further disadvantage of this method is the fact that, as 8mm and Super 8 sound projectors are scarce, a sound tape still has to be made to be used for exhibition purposes where there is no suitable projector.

A third way to add sound is to use a cassette designed to both record in synchronization with the camera and to play in synchronization with the projector. This device, available on several cameras and matched projectors, makes possible effective on-the-spot reporting, but the quality of the sound is often limited by the effectiveness of the recorder.

Music is all that is needed for the sound track of some films. Children are quick to see how music can set a mood and will search diligently for just the right selections to match the continuity of their films — and they incidentally become familiar with music that they otherwise might not listen to. Sound editing becomes even more exciting when voice-over-music or sound-over-music extends the possibilities of the sound track. Because tape can be erased and rerun, experimenting with sound in the classroom has none of the finality of shooting with the camera. Working with three tape recorders, sound gathered "on location" — street noise, boat whistles, conversation, sirens, etc. — can be combined with music or combined with speech. Children can explore the possibilities of sound by making their own sound effects, by playing musical scores on their own instruments, by using choral speech, by conducting interviews, by extending sound (on some tape recorders) with echo chambers and tone controls, and by the use of deliberate discord and atonality. Continuous effects can be achieved by replacing the usual full reel of tape with a tape loop containing a sound sequence that keeps playing over and over. This loop can be played at different speeds.

Fascinating results can be obtained by using an "orchestra" of tape recorders — one recording while the others play. Several layers of sound can be recorded at the same time to create rich sound textures and unusual effects. The same loop, for example, can be recorded at various speeds, at different tonal levels, and with fresh sound fed in whenever appropriate.

When a piece of music, a poem, a selection of sounds, or a rhythmic pattern becomes the basis for a film the usual editing pattern is reversed: the film is cut to conform to the sound. In this case, film episodes and sound interludes are often timed to conform to each other so that the montage of images matches the montage of sounds.

Tape, like films, can be edited and spliced. Tape splicers that facilitate the cutting and joining of lengths of film with pressure-sensitive tape are inexpensive and easy to operate. Editing tape in a selection of colors makes the storing of more than one sound track on a reel practical. For example, using a length of red tape to precede one sound track, a length of yellow to precede another, and so on, will make it simple to match films and tapes when projecting.

Some children become fascinated with the possibilities of the tape recorder and want to experiment with sound on its own. Such youngsters should be encouraged to develop original tapes, independent of films, that can always be used to advantage as incidental "program music" between screenings at a school film festival.

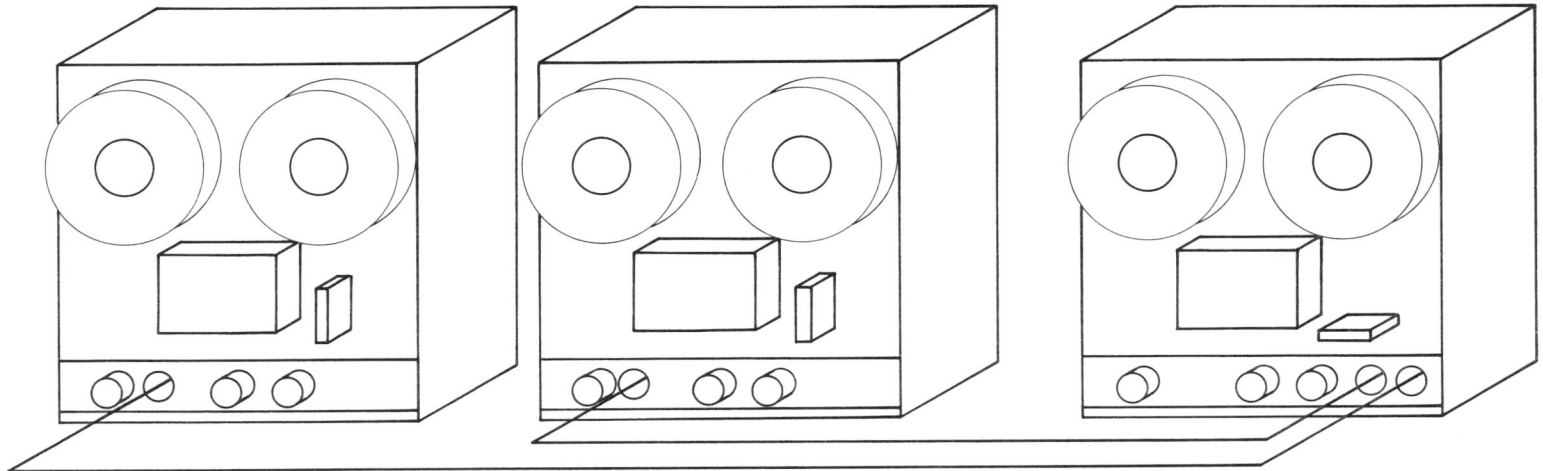

By using three tape recorders, speech from one tape can be combined with music from another to make a third composite tape.

ANIMATION AND TITLING

While working from reality, in and out of school, has the advantage of bringing children into meaningful contact with their world, films using "still" subject matter extend the scope of film making in other worthwhile ways. They provide motivation for all kinds of visual research and give youngsters an opportunity to use art skills and art materials.

Three-dimensional materials, such as puppets, models, household articles, furniture, toys and so on, and two-dimensional materials, such as photographs, paintings, and cartoons, can be the basis of films that are as exciting, provocative, and moving as those made from real life. "Animation" is very much a part of professional film making and in many ways is more sophisticated cinema than nonanimated film. Much of the vivacity and appeal of today's TV commercials is due to animation, some of it so subtle that it passes as live footage, while the visual impact of much fine film titling is almost entirely due to animation and the skillful use of still material.

The principles of animation are based on the way "movies" work. In ordinary use the 8mm or Super 8 camera shoots 18 (or 24) single frames per second in sequence. Each frame is a single picture, and if the camera or subject is moving, then each picture is slightly different. The human eye can clearly see a single frame when it is projected at 18 frames per second, but the image tends to remain in the mind so that the change of position in the next frame over-registers in such a smooth way as to give the impression of continuous action. Children readily understand this principle of animation when the old-fashioned flip book is used for demonstration. The teacher might take a small pad and draw a simple figure on a back page and on each preceding page trace the figure with slight but significant changes in the action, i.e., an arm rising up and down or a figure walking. When the pages of the pad are flipped the figure will appear to move. The faster the pages are flipped, obviously, the quicker the figure appears to move. The children should also notice that the more drawings there are, with shorter distances between the action, the longer and smoother the gesture appears to be.

While the flip book is helpful for demonstration, the children will wish to explore the potential of the actual film. Drawing on 16mm film always provides youngsters with an exciting and effective experience in animation, and because so little equipment is required it is one of the simplest projects for the film-making teacher. Only film and a projector are necessary.

16mm film is preferable, because each frame provides a larger working area than 8mm. Clear film is desirable but is harder to get than leader film or old, discarded developed film. 16mm leader in 100-foot lengths is relatively cheap, and easy to obtain, but the teacher should take care to get the nonplastic type with an emulsion on one side. School audiovisual departments usually have old film they wish to discard, and TV stations daily throw away hundreds of feet of suitable 16mm film. The film emulsion can be scraped off for brief flashes of light or line drawings, or the emulsion containing the image can be removed with bleach, lacquer thinner, rubber cement thinner, or profilm adhering liquid. This is not necessary for leader film. Here the emulsion can be scratched for special light effects.

Children can work on the film with magic markers, acrylic inks, and india inks. On the 16mm film the picture frame lies between the two sprocket holes. It is possible to write (backwards) or to draw on each frame in such a way that the image will move much as it did in the flip book. Students often animate a dot or line by moving its position slightly from frame to frame over the rhythms of lines and textures created by scratching, printing, or painting with various tools. Children can create as freely as they do on paper, disregarding frames at some times, recognizing them at others. When such film is projected (at the silent speed setting) and accompanied by quick and bouncy music the students are amazed and pleased at the results; many become so enthusiastic with the hand-worked film that they concentrate on it to the exclusion of other kinds of film making.

77

Filmed animation works much the same way. To give a very simple example, a student wishing to show a bouncing colored ball would cut out a round piece of colored paper and place it on a different-colored background. Using the single frame release on a fixed camera, he would shoot two frames of the ball, then move the ball a fraction of an inch and shoot another two frames, repeating these sequences until the ball has bounced its way out of the picture. The youngster can control the speed of the ball by the number of frames he shoots (usually up to five or six for slow-motion) and the distance he moves the ball at each position. Too many frames or too big a move will spoil the illusion and make the motion jerky. Variations on the circle theme are only as limited as the student's imagination — different colors, different shapes, dividing and then reuniting the shapes — are just the beginning of the possibilities. One group of eighth-grade girls romanticized the circle: the male and female circles blushed when they came into contact or turned green with jealousy when one contacted some other circle. Abstract materials such as colored pins, clay, macaroni, beans, toothpicks, and silver foil can be used for similar effects. Diagrams and cartoons can appear as if they are magically drawn before the viewers' eyes. The artist draws a brief section, shooting two or three frames, then draws another section, and so on. Collage images culled from magazines can form a good basis for animation. One or more selected face structures combined with different additional eyes and mouths can alternately open and close in a series of frames. The rather disturbing images which result then appear to blink or to talk. Cutouts of the film maker's own art work make equally successful film. Paper planes can zoom about on a painted sky in a classic dogfight, with a sound track of the roar of motors and the rattle of machine guns. Tracer bullets may appear and suddenly and literally one of the planes may catch fire and actually burn its way out of the picture. A series of nonmoving drawings or paintings can provide the camera with the means to "tell" an engrossing film.

Three-dimensional animation is equally effective. When consideration is given to the camera angle and the lighting, then clay, silver foil, crumpled paper, blocks, and models can become "alive" and perform in such a manner as to delight all children. Twenty-two lumps of clay in two different colors become a football game. A castle grows magically from blocks in front of the viewers' eyes and disappears as mysteriously.

Commercial animation usually depends on the overlap of identically sized acetate sheets and requires skill and precision. Children's animation, on the other hand, can be magical and carefree, and it is as successful in the primary and pre-school years as in the high school. With young children, the teacher is largely responsible for the technical operation of the camera and the lighting, and the children are free to click the single-frame release and to manipulate the subjects of their choice; in the upper grades, students can control all these steps themselves.

The cardinal rule of animation is that the camera must remain fixed in position. In order to foster the illusion of motion the camera itself should be as immovable as possible, and a good stable animation stand is desirable. The animation stand must have a base plate on which the camera is bolted, pointing downward. The base plate should be positioned so that the lens of the camera will be centered in the stand. The stand should be high enough (usually four feet or higher unless the camera has a close-up lens attached) so that the camera can focus on objects set on the platform at the bottom of the stand. Some stands have platforms that can be adjusted at different heights, but this seems unnecessary for children if the

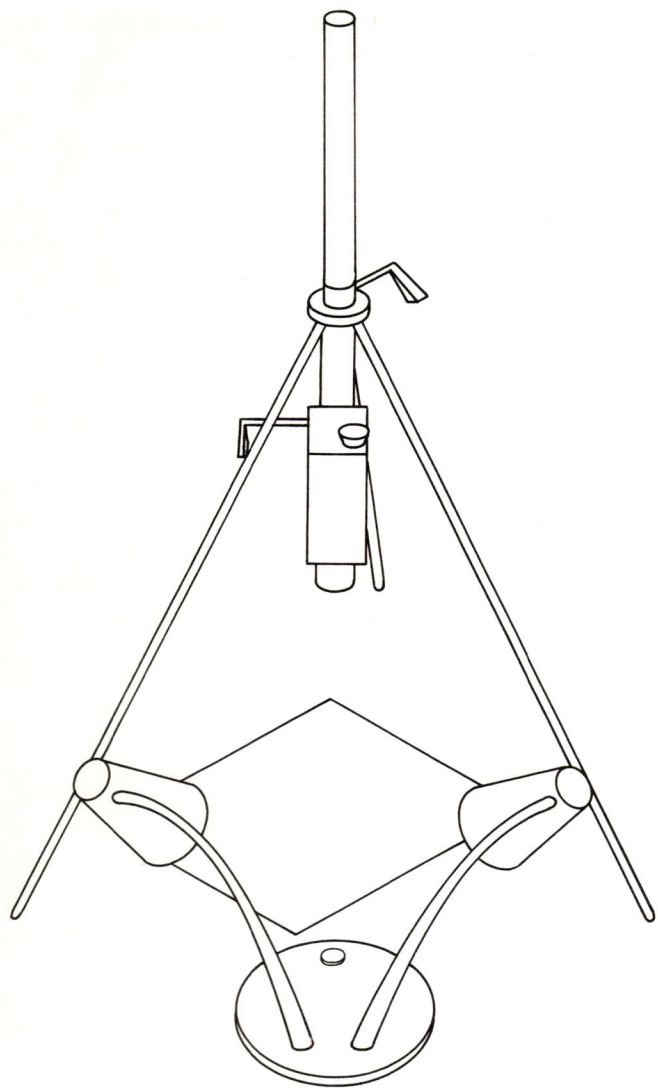

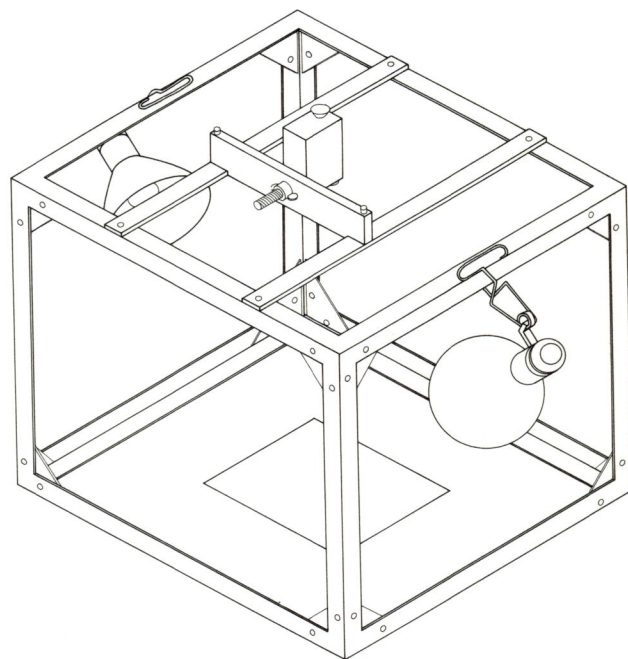

camera has a zoom lens. The animation stand should also have some kind of support for at least two attached lights and a small step ladder so that smaller children can see what they are shooting. Animation stands should be broadly based so that they are not easily tipped or jarred. The main fault with the tripod in animation is the frequency with which children trip on its legs. We have, however, shown one here with a close-up lens attached as an alternative when no animation stand is available. Note that even ordinary lights will work if there is enough illumination to satisfy the light meter. An equally useful alternative is the Kodak Flexiclamp — a flexible wing-nut support that will fix the camera on a firm surface, for example a high table or desk, so it may shoot downward or at an angle. (In the photograph, the camera is clamped to a stepladder.) Lights can also be clamped to the table support.

The procedure for animation outlined on pages 82-84 is designed to shoot two-dimensional material on a flat surface at the bottom of a fixed animation stand. If the student desires to film three-dimensional animation, the camera and lighting should be angled so that the subject appears at its best angle. In this instance, a tripod or Flexiclamp is often easier to work with. The teacher can handle the more difficult technical steps when working with younger children, a task that will not prove too demanding as once the focus and lights are set they usually remain constant throughout most of the shooting.

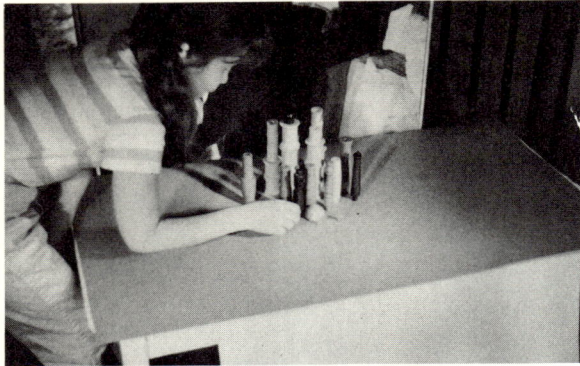

Animation Procedure

1. Choose a subject and gather the material necessary for filming. Once a student starts filming he should endeavor to shoot as many whole sequences as he can. The camera cannot be moved, and as there are usually other students waiting to use the camera and stand, this is no time for the youngster to wander off to search for more material or ideas. It usually takes between three and five hours to shoot a reel or cartridge. It is therefore wise to organize the shooting routine. Younger children become bored if required to work for more than an hour. It is usually better to have them work in twos or threes, one moving the subject and the other clicking off the single frames. An hour's work usually results in about a minute of filmed animation. The next group could take over the unused portion of the film, and any further work by the original group can be spliced onto the developed film later.

2. Set the first sequence by laying out the background color and props on the shooting platform. It is best to cover the whole platform with the base color (or a neutral gray, close in value to the base color) even though parts of the platform might be outside the camera viewing area. The lighting on the entire platform must be the same as the light on the picture area or the light meter tends to give an incorrect reading.

3. Load and check the camera, then fasten it firmly to the base plate. If necessary, draw a line or fix a piece of tape on the base plate or similarly mark the tripod's legs so the camera position can be corrected if jarred. Attach a single-frame-release cable (a long cable is very useful, because it enables the children to shoot frames while still crouched near the filming board).

4. Check the focus by zooming in (see pages 32-33), then zoom back to the desired framing distance. It is necessary

to move the background and props to correspond with the camera's viewfinder. When the background is "set" properly in the viewfinder it should be registered. This can be done by fastening down cardboard strips as in silkscreening so that different backgrounds of the same size can be substituted. Children often accidentally shift them so it is best to tape them down firmly. Many cameras shoot, at this range, a picture slightly larger than their viewfinder would indicate, so it is wise to inspect the perimeter of the viewer carefully for tapes or edges that might still be visible, then to zoom away slightly to make sure.

5. Set the lights. The best type of lights for animation are photofloods. These can be installed in relatively cheap clamp-ons. The lamps themselves are expensive and last only three or four hours but give the best light on the subject. Movie lights are also suitable. So are spot lights, floodlights, and tensor high-intensity lamps, although the light meter will give a much lower reading with these. All these lights, but particularly the photofloods and movie lights, get very hot and should be turned off as often as possible. Children should be warned not to touch them. It is quite possible, even preferable, to use daylight or natural light if the stand is in an advantageous position to receive enough diffused lighting from the windows. The lights, usually two, should be set at a position laterally to the left and right of the camera and tilted so they shoot down at the film platform at an angle of about 45 degrees. Good lighting is an even coverage of the picture with no hot spots (concentrated light) and no reflected light coming directly back to the camera. If the light is too irregular the lights should be moved back, or bounced off white surfaces onto the platform, or a third flood-type light added to blend them. This extra light, if needed, could be attached on the upper support nearest the top of the camera. Light reflecting back into the camera lens can obliterate the image on the film, and care should be taken to adjust the lights and the shiny parts of the subject matter so that there is no danger of this happening. Usually the lighting angle of 45 degrees is sufficient. Care should also be taken to avoid cast shadows such as those from the animation stand's supports, the release cable, or the edges of the subject on the filming board. Special effects can be achieved through the manipulation of the lights. Colored acetates or "gels" can be attached to one or both lamps; moving lights can particularly dramatize three-dimensional animation; or the bottom platform can be translucent with lights placed below. But whenever a light change is used the light meter must be reset.

6. Set the manual override to stabilize the meter setting. When the lights are set and on, depress the camera's trigger halfway and take a reading from the automatic light meter (see pages 29-30). Switch the automatic meter to manual and hand-set the same reading. This is a must for the single-frame-release mechanism and insures a constant and regular light in the animated film. This light-meter setting process must be repeated with each change in the base color of the background or in the lighting, but can remain constant throughout the major part of the filming. (So, of course, can the focus, with only the zoom in use to change framing distances.)

7. Shoot film. The beginning film maker will be amazed and somewhat upset at how quickly the hours that he spent in shooting can speed through the projector. But on the second or third viewing he usually forgets the long effort in the joy of seeing the transformation of his inanimate objects into "live "shapes and creatures. The young film maker finds in animation an extension of his ability to control his world.

Titling Techniques

Not all school films need titles, but when it is decided to add title and end sections, any of the film-making techniques discussed so far can be pressed into service. Animation, superimposition, and straight shooting all lend themselves to the creation of impressive titles. A title can be extremely simple, traced out with a stick in the smooth, sandy surface of a beach, chalked on a fence, or crayoned on a piece of cardboard; or it can be a technical *tour de force* involving complicated animation or the superimposition of letters over movement. Whatever its form, it should reflect the mood and spirit of the film to which it relates and its style should be in keeping with its format. Particularly in short films, titling data should be brief and its layout should make it easy to read.

While a title is too often a film routine that the audience puts up with while waiting for the film itself to begin, there is no reason why it cannot be as appealing and provocative as any other part of a movie. In today's cinema, titling is taken seriously and some films are remembered as much for their titles as for their content. The titles of school films should be no less significant.

A title not only gives information about a film, it sets the mood, so it is important that its content should be consistent with the film's purpose. Styles of lettering should be carefully considered. The art treatment must reflect the general feeling of the film and the entire conception should have a rhythm and pace characteristic of the production. With children, these qualities are most often achieved when titling is done with techniques appropriate to the age group making the film. Titles for a film by ten-year-olds, for example, should have titles that reflect the art of ten-year-olds. Here, free lettering with poster paint

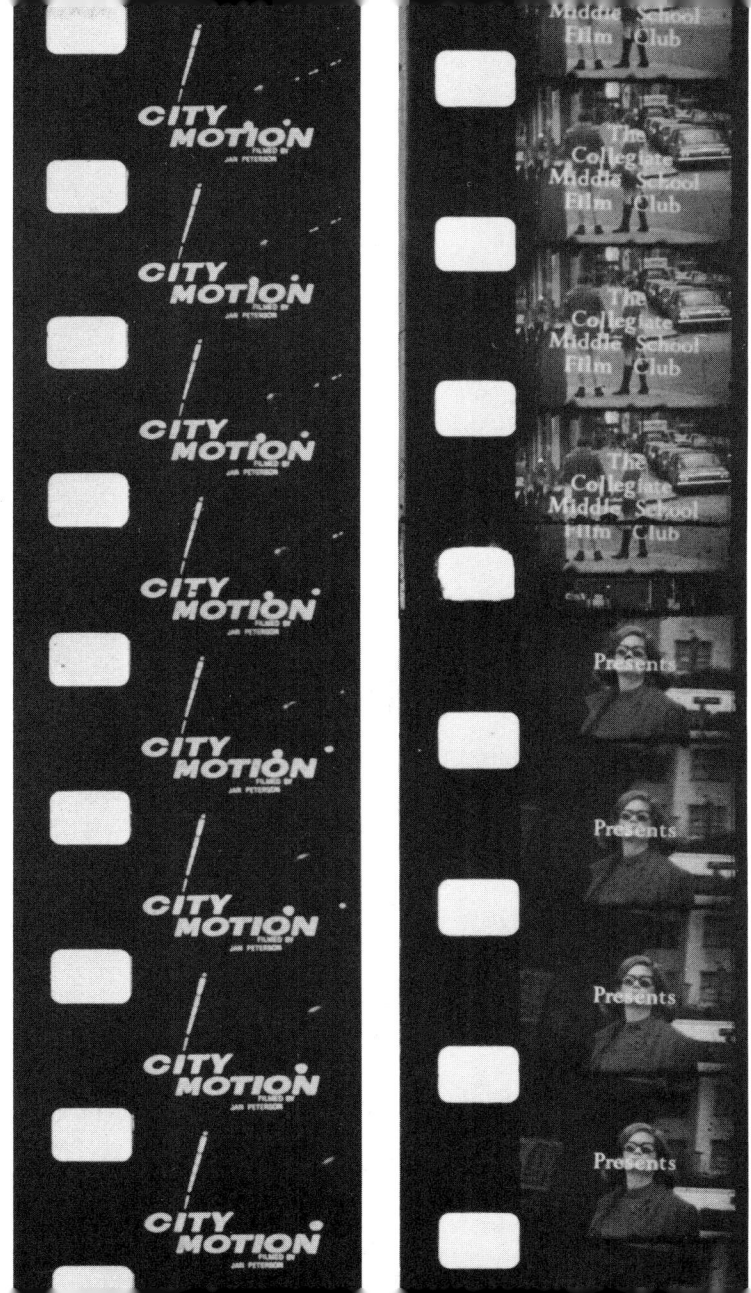

on sheets of colored construction paper is more likely to produce appropriate titling than commercial letters carefully spaced on a titling board. With younger children it is often wise to dispense with titles altogether or to use spoken titles.

The placing of a film title in the sequence of a film should be done as freely as any other aspect of editing. Most often, titling will be most effective when it precedes the rest of the film, but there are times when this format is not appropriate. If an unusual placement of a title is necessary to draw particular attention to its significance, then it is best to break with tradition. Sometimes involving the audience in a story line or establishing a mood before the title appears will be more successful than the usual titles-before-action format.

Contrast can be used to good effect in titling without destroying the consistency that should exist between title and content. Black-and-white titles might provide a welcome diversity when used with a film in color; animated cartoon figures in the title of a comedy might point up the humor of its real characters, abstract designs in the title of a film about the city might contrast with images of actual buildings yet convey feelings of their geometric construction.

All the animated techniques work well for titling, and even the simplest devices, such as adding one letter at a time until a credit is complete, are surprisingly effective on the screen. Whatever technique is used for the title, it should reflect in the treatment of the end credits so that an artistic unity is established.

Children, especially in the upper grades, enjoy the simple but effective technology that goes into making titles superimposed over film action. Such titles are particularly effective when lettering appears over filmed material that is part of a continuing story line on the screen. For example, an airplane can be seen landing; as it lands the titles appear superimposed over it; the titles disappear as its passengers begin to disembark; and the camera zooms in to a close-up of the two principals of the film. Such titles can only be made in single 8, 8mm, and 16mm cameras in which the film can be rolled back. Several simple steps are involved in making a superimposed title.

1. White (or any color that will show up crisply against black) letters are adhered to a nonreflective black background. The titles shown on page 86 were made from white pressure-sensitive letters placed on a sheet of black TV board (obtainable in most art stores). At least 12 inches of black should extend beyond the letters on all sides to ensure that only the letters and their black surround will register on the film. Painted or chalked letters or letters cut from magazines or construction paper will prove satisfactory as long as they contrast with the black and are not so elaborate in style that they are difficult to read over moving images.

2. The various sections of the titling — title, names of actors and cameramen, etc. — must be shot separately, and, if the action over which they are to be superimposed is continuous, shot in the order in which they will be shown.

3. The film is rolled back (without being "flipped") on the reel on which it was originally wound, precautions being taken to shield it from the light.

4. Now the film is reshot, the action over which the titles and credits are to appear being exposed.

Regardless of what film technique is used to create a title, the sensitivity and appropriateness of its art content will affect its visual impact. The least complicated approach, a title spelled out in pebbles, for instance, deserves as much artistic consideration as one involving expensive and complicated materials. Making use of art materials and processes with which children are already familiar can often suggest ideas to them that grow out of art activities they have enjoyed.

Lettering, of course, plays an important role in titling and is an area that should be thoroughly explored. While some children are very adept at producing either innovative or traditional lettering with paints, crayons, chalks, inks, or colored papers that is both handsome and easy to read, others are more at home cutting out and manipulating "found" alphabets from magazines or arranging prepared lettering. Titling kits are not recommended, because of their limited range of alphabets, but pressure-sensitive lettering, which is available in many styles, colors, and sizes, is excellent.

"Sarah's Story"—an Animated Film

Film is capable of controlling to a large extent what we perceive and how we perceive it. The camera is able to focus and direct our eyes as it analyzes its subject. A good example of this is the difference in the way one sees a work of fine art and the way one sees a film of the same work of art. The camera usually tells a considerably different story from the original, and if directed with sensibility and intelligence it can offer great insights. The linear-sequential nature of film structures the art experience in a different manner than did the original work. In fact, the camera can actually create a new work of art evolving from another already established art form.

The art work on these five pages was taken from a series of eighteen paintings done with felt-tip pens by a six-year-old girl. Although everyone who saw the pictures was very curious, Sarah did not volunteer any explanation or give any story line until her parents decided to help her film the series. When the paintings were all laid out, two

versions of "How the Princess Helped the Poor People" were taped. These were the basis of a scenario, and Sarah placed the pictures in sequence and gave directions for filming. She very quickly understood that the camera could select just part of a painting and relate that part to another part of the same picture or to another painting. For example, she picked out the angels from different pictures and shot them in sequence and in different sizes for one part of her story line. Her taped script was vividly visual and suggested many ways to film the sequences. Sarah shot some of the film from the animation stand and directed the rest. When the developed film returned and had been briefly edited, Sarah retaped her story to correspond with the film, using a little dubbed music to give dramatic emphasis. Only a small selection of her paintings and parts of her tapes can be shown here, but they should give some idea of the possibilities of this approach — and the fun her parents had doing the film with her.

Why I named it "How the Princess Helped the Poor People" is because it kind of goes like that. She looks over and sees the poor people and she looks over again and again in the film 'cause my dad put it like that with the camera so that a person could really see how she was looking at the poor people.

This is the story of the princess and the poor people. It's kind of how the princess helped the poor people. You see, she comes and sees the poor people kind of wandering through the woods sadly, without any clothes, and their babies. Some of their babies have cuts and they're sick or something because they can't afford anything to get them better. Now, she comes to them, nicely, and helps one of the mothers to help her child and she says, "Here, this will help it." And she gives it a little medicine to make him feel better. And then, after she helps the mother, she meets everybody in the whole group and she tells them, "Tomorrow at sunrise, at early dawn, come here and wait here at this flower." And she sings a little song and a beautiful, gigantic, beautiful, big flower — the prettiest flower in the world — just up, came up out of the ground.

"Meet here at this flower. Do not worry. You can go as far as you want because you will see the flower anytime as the flower will carry the beautifulest light in the world."

And they could see this beautiful light out, that they could see over the treetops. And then the princess wandered off and she said, "Remember. Meet at dawn. At dawn the flower will be a pink light instead of this beautiful kind of orange."

So they go away, apart.

But the princess remembers that she has a scarf and a couple of little tiny dresses in her bundle. She gives them the dresses because she knows that her father does not know what she carries in her bundle, just little tiny dresses, not royal dresses.

This is one of the fairies, the queen fairy, that's come down to take care of them. She's brought two pairs of clothes and she just wiggles her wand a little bit and a spell appears on the tree. And it starts swaying back and forth and making lovely sounds and singing a song and the tree grew out a bell so that it could play while it sang. ["Oh, terrific!" said Mom. "Yes," said Sarah. "Imagination."]

Sarah

And if we see angels in the story, those are because the princéss sends the angels to come and help take care of the poor people.

Well, you see, the mother is real old. She's — well, she's just died, because — it's her time to die. The angels have come to look after the little girl and the baby. Those beautiful colors in the trees, well, they are just kind of design, imaginations, you know. The little girl and the baby can't see them but the angels can see them, because the angels kind of make them, shine, sort of, on there.

This is a little girl, say her age is about seven, and this is her bigger sister, and this is a bigger sister, and they have a little baby. You see their mother is down picking flowers where you can't see her and they are following her down and are going to pick flowers. Whenever they go past now, the flowers appear. The princess, the poor people, everyone, flowers appear, kind of imagination. And the flowers burst up and stay there forever.

"US" — A SIXTH-GRADE FILM PROJECT

Here are excerpts from a sixth-grade film that demonstrates just how feasible it is for any teacher, with or without equipment or special skills, to work in film making with his class. "US" was made with borrowed equipment (two 16mm cameras, an editor, and a splicer), and the class raised the money for film and processing. The teacher had had no experience in film making, although he obtained outside advice.

While "US" is an artistic effort in that images were arranged in an aesthetic as well as a meaningful order and the sound track was similarly inspired, it is a record, too — a modest piece of reportage that provides insights about a real-life situation in a way that only a film can do. In some ways "US" could be thought of as a social-studies project. It was made at a time when the sixth grade, along with three or four other grades, was occupying temporary quarters in what had been part of a hotel, while a new addition was being added to the school itself. It is the only account that documents this era of the school's history.

Once the class had decided on its subject, the film's organization was, of course, pretty straightforward. Shooting assignments were worked out, each concerned with one aspect of the school day. Camera teams of two or three boys each were given the responsibility of filming such scenes as the school bus arriving, lunch being served, the study hall.

A period was devoted to learning to work the cameras, and some time was spent discussing shooting techniques. As this was a first film, a simple approach was stressed that emphasized three basic shots — long shots, close-ups of individuals, and slow pans. Everyone practiced hand-holding the rather heavy cameras and using a tripod. Because the borrowed Bolexes were the older nonreflex models, time had to be spent teaching the class how to use the lens turrets and make parallax adjustments — rather complicated teaching procedures that can be avoided altogether when reflex 8mm and Super 8 cameras are used.

A light meter was required and the class had to learn how to read and use it, another time-consuming detail that can be avoided by the use of 8mm and Super 8 cameras. Two photoflood bulbs bounced light off ceilings and walls for interior lighting. These were often hand-held by students so that the camera could be moved freely around halls and classrooms. At times, auxiliary floods were needed to illuminate larger areas for long shots.

In no time the class became very adept at improvising procedures so that the camera could keep up with whatever action was going on. Shooting from odd angles, from ladders, getting lights into difficult positions, even guessing at exposures quite accurately, all became routine. Everyone had a chance to shoot some footage, but as the film progressed it was obvious that some students enjoyed shooting more than others, some preferred working on technical arrangements, some acting.

Eventually the basic scenes were recorded and the film processed. Now the class was able to see the results of their efforts. Poor footage was edited out, and the rest was divided up into sections, labeled, and hung from a length of cord stretched across the classroom. Then it was put together with masking tape into an order of sorts that more or less reconstructed the school day. So far everything had been, on the whole, straight reportage.

Now titles and credits were decided upon, a beginning and an ending were contrived, and various intermediate scenes to keep the action moving along were developed. All these episodes were rehearsed and eventually filmed. This footage was processed, previewed, and edited into the original sequential arrangement, again with masking tape. This taped-together version was then taken by a small group of students who, using the editor, splicer, and dry-press splices, spliced the rough-edited lengths of film into the final film story. As they did this, they interspersed footage from certain scenes, such as the school bell being rung, students crowding through the halls, which had been purposely overshot to strengthen continuity.

When the complete film, including the titles and credits, was spliced, it was projected and a sound track worked out. The sound was kept simple; basically, electronic Bach to accompany classroom scenes and popular music for out-of-classroom episodes, both relieved by the sound of the school bell recorded to mark the change of classes. The film was not striped; it was designed to be shown in conjunction with a synchronized tape.

"US" starts with a shot of the entrance to the school, and the only dialogue in the film, "There once was a quiet little school on West 86th Street." The school buses arrive and the students enter the school.

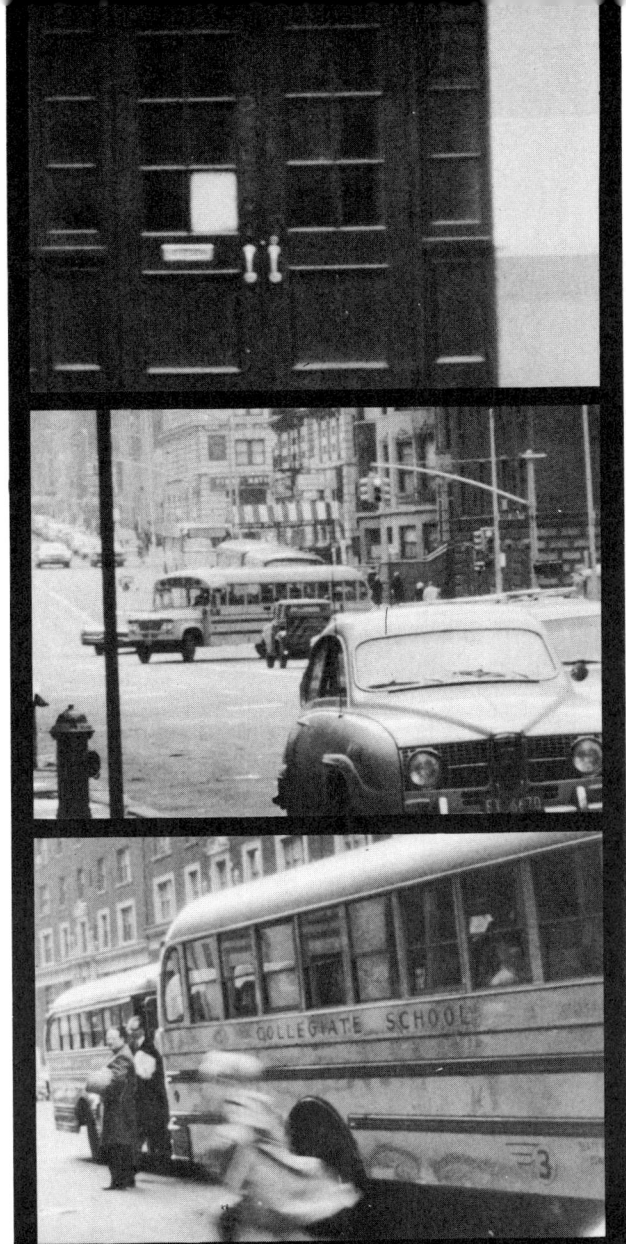

95

As soon as they are all inside, strange things begin to happen. Books sail out of windows, students appear in odd places where they normally wouldn't be. Then boys start escaping out of windows and have to be herded back into the school again. Eventually the last escapee is captured and the school day starts.

Now come the titles. So that the pace of the film will be maintained we see them being made. First the title itself, US then THOUGHT UP BY US, FILMED BY US, and finally AND ALL ABOUT US. Another credit, not shown here, read FILMED BY US, SOUND BY US, EDITED BY US. The bell announces the first period. A series of scenes, only suggested here, shows what goes on in various morning classes of the school. The bell rings again, this time for the lunch break.

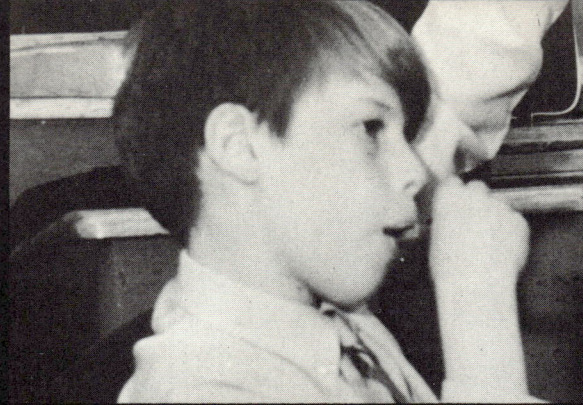

The film concentrates in its final scenes on the class who made it. Most of its episodes are not shown here, but these few frames give some idea of its atmosphere and continuity. Among sequences featuring sports, dramatics, and other school activities is this one of an English period. We see studies of the teacher and the reactions to his questions by individuals and by the whole class. No acting or filming scripts were used; all action was spontaneous.

Eventually, the school day comes to an end. The boys rush to catch their buses. The classroom, only a few minutes ago so full of life, is now quiet. The head of the school locks up and disappears down 86th Street (up which the buses had come at the beginning of the film). We return to the empty classroom and hear the school bell echoing through the deserted hallways.

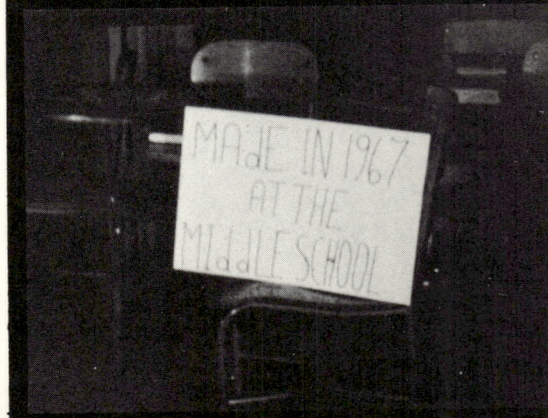

MADE IN 1967
AT THE
MIDDLE SCHOOL

CREATIVE FILM PRESENTATION

There is no reason why a youngster must be committed to the conventional theater-house type of presentation of movies. Instead of one movie at a time on a single central screen, the children often create quite different environments using multiple screens and mixed media. Students discover many different types of reflecting surfaces for projecting their films, ranging from the traditional glass-bead screen to large weather balloons. Other projection surfaces could be three-dimensional screens, gyrating white robed figures against a white background, architectural structures, kinetic mobile-like shapes, or translucent plastics and papers. Multiple screening of a group of movies on a multi-faceted three-dimensional screen can create a new and quite different total out of individual components. A student film that was just an incomplete fragment now makes a significant contribution to the visual impression. For example, if there has been an outstanding event like a storm during the class shooting period quite a few students will have footage of the weather and its effects. When these are shown simultaneously the visual experience is quite different and probably richer than showing them individually in sequence. Slides and projected light effects that have evolved from contemporary light shows can also be used with movies. Due to the nature of projected light, however, it is very difficult to superimpose one projected image onto another. It is better to isolate the images or to block out one of the images at the point where they overlap. Slides and hand-drawn film are easier to block out, and a student, for example, may choose to show a multi-media multi-imaged film by having a 16mm hand-drawn film as the general textural ground. He would place the projector well back in the room so that a large image is screened. Then, by using two 8mm projectors which have been placed nearer to the screen, the student projects two different aspects of a theme into areas that have been carefully opaqued out on each 16mm frame. A series of slides or the light table of the overhead projector can be similarly opaqued in selected areas for the same effect. The use of magic lanterns, strobe lights, polaroid lenses, and other projected light media combined with films is just beginning to be explored.

Film Festivals

While film showings in the classroom and at school assemblies give student films a certain kind of exposure, an evening set aside for a film festival has added advantages that should not be overlooked. Such an evening is worthwhile if only to give parents and friends who might not be able to attend a daytime screening a chance to participate. When a number of films are to be shown in a comprehensive manner, it is worth taking time to prepare program notes, and to rehearse the technical aspects of the screening so that, if tape recorders are to be used, sound and image are properly coordinated. A festival, too, sets an exciting deadline, often badly needed, for those students who benefit from a goal to aim at in completing their films and marks the end of a film-making year with an auspicious occasion.

Children should play the major role in every aspect of the planning and presentation of a festival. There are always some students who enjoy working with projectors and tape recorders more than any other phase of film making, and here they can be given every opportunity to put their enthusiasms to good use. Nothing can detract more from one's enjoyment of an evening's films than technical hitches in projection and faulty sound synchronization. The complete program should be thoroughly rehearsed and every piece of equipment checked and rechecked. Sending out invitations, making posters, selling tickets, ushering, lighting, and handing out programs are all jobs that students can do to make them feel a real part of the festival.

An evening of student films, including, as it should, work from every member of a group, must be carefully programmed if it is to hold the attention of an audience used to attending professional movies. If a large number of films have been produced during the year it is a good idea to break the evening with a generous intermission when refreshments might be served or, at least, when members of the audience can walk around and chat among themselves and with the students.

If there are too many films to show all of them in their entirety, it is perhaps best to show some full-length and screen only excerpts from others. There should be no hint of competition as to which films will be excerpted; rather, some sort of logical decision-making must be instituted. For example, films which still need editing, or are otherwise not quite completed, would lend themselves to excerpting and can be shown complete at some later date.

The screening order should be carefully prepared so that its variety is emphasized: some animated films can be shown as part of each half of the program, films made by younger children can be interspersed with those of older students, and so on.

A film festival is meant to do more than provide an evening's entertainment. It should provide convincing evidence that children feel deeply about the films they make; it should impress parents with the educational benefits of film making. If there are not too many items on the program it is a good idea to have each film maker say a few words about his film. When this does not seem practical, it is still wise to have each student acknowledge the applause for his efforts.

An annotated program in which each student puts down a few words about his film helps the audience to understand the implications of each offering, particularly those films which are untitled and have no dialogue. The following are excerpts from an actual festival program (of the Collegiate Middle School Film Club) that not only indicate the number and variety of films a group can produce in a school year but give an idea of the type of statements youngsters — in this case junior high school students — make about their films.

John Rossant: DREAM   In this film I tried to simulate a dream. I tried to make it Daliesque and surrealistic. I used the same techniques as I used in *Pages from the Diary of a Mad Man* but *Dream* has more of a narrative value.

Allen Low: WHEELS   This is a film about wheels, moving and still. I used a Super 8 Kodak M6 to make this film.

Jan Peterson: CITY MOTION   This was filmed at night entirely in or after a rain storm. I used Type A 8mm film. I tried to vary my shots as much as possible and to make use of the lights of the city at night to record this special motion of the city. I filmed through a telephone booth, for example, and focused on the raindrops that were clinging to the glass so that the lights in the background were out of focus and moving.

Peter Stoneham: EXCERPTS   An animated film which is a collection of short parts acted out by assorted Plasticene figures.

Tim Moore: RAMBLER OF LIFE (assisted by Jan Peterson and Tony Stewart)   The movie is based on parts of a six-page poem that I wrote last year at school. The poem is about a person walking along the beach and thinking about what has affected his life. I wrote this poem to try and find out what life is about for me. The movie was filmed on the beach at Fire Island, in New York City, and indoors. The poem is the sound track for the movie and I have background music from Benjamin Britten, the Beatles, and Vaughan Williams.

James Madden: LONELINESS   In this film I started out to express my feelings of loneliness. When I had finished my film it did turn out lonely and desolate as I showed familiar scenes of normally crowded buildings, roads, and worksites all deserted. I felt that this was the atmosphere of loneliness.

Tony Stewart: THE AMERICAN MURDER   An analogy of American murder movies. It contains all the visual clichés of most murder movies, although some are not as apparent as others. It was filmed partly as a spoof, partly as a protest, but mainly as an experiment. The purpose was to see what could be done in the way of story telling with silent 8mm equipment.

Peter Grunwald and Steve Tucker: BOOK DAY   This movie was made in about two weeks. We collected the different scenes in the library and blended them into a comedy. There were scenes of last year's Book Day and of the mothers struggling to make it possible. Aside from the comedy, it was a documentary and a commercial.

John Rossant: PAGES FROM THE DIARY OF A MAD-MAN   In this film I try to capture a few minutes of what might be a trip on hallucinogens or a look into the minds and wanderings of deranged persons. One technique I used was using short unrelated film sequences, not for their narrative value, but for their symbolic and graphic value. Another technique I used was coloring the processed film frame by frame.

Tom White: WINDOWS   I have taken shots of all types of windows. I went looking for unusual windows in usual places and regular windows in unusual places.

Steven Tucker: CHRISTMAS IN NEW YORK   This movie is a collection of all the things that make up the Christmas season in New York. Nearly all of the editing of this film was done right in the camera.

Tony Hodes: EXPRESSION   To make *Expression* I used an 8mm Bolex P9. It is a series of sequences, some animation and some simulated psychedelic effects. The special effects were created by arranging colored lights in different patterns to reflect off different materials revolving on a record-player turntable.

Chris Finney: TREES AND LEAVES One roll of this film was taken in the autumn when all the leaves were different colors. The second roll was taken during the winter. There are about thirteen colorful paintings taken on the first roll which are mixed with the roll of autumn leaves. When I filmed the still pictures I zoomed in on different parts of the paintings. I contrasted the paintings with the real trees.

Christian Steinway: HEIGHTS The reason I made this film about heights is to show the magnificent beauty of tall objects when in the right perspective.

Peter Grunwald: MOROCCO This film is the result of a Christmas trip to Morocco. We spent most of our time in the market places, giving me the time and the opportunity to make this movie. It all had to be done in color to catch all the color of the market places.

James Galef: THE SHOW This is an animated movie done frame by frame with clay figures. It is a collection of fourteen acts with an announcer. This film was taken on Mars and the announcer will speak to you through mental telepathy.

Arthur Levitt: GIRLS In making this film we used some of the techniques of Candid Camera, trying to see how girls would react in unusual situations.

Chris Woods: NEW YORK This film was taken from the 16th floor or above of two or three different buildings in New York. I went looking for reflections and weird patterns.

Steven Elliot and Tom Hayes: THE SKYSCRAPER This movie was based on a poem written by Carl Sandburg. The poem was written about Chicago but fits New York perfectly.

Randy West: KID! This movie concerns a murder committed by a boy. He's seen at the crime by an extortionist. The rest of the film deals with the way he pays the blackmailer.

Three groups are needed to handle the physical aspects of the program — one for projection, one for sound, and one for lighting. Identical cue sheets should be prepared for each individual in each group and for whoever is coordinating the events of the evening. These sheets should contain the following information:

1. The order in which the films will be shown (each film being numbered accordingly).
2. The category of each film — 8mm, Super 8, or 16mm — and how long it takes to run.
3. A color cue for each film to indicate the location of its sound track on one of the evening's master tapes.
4. A revolution counter number to mark which point to start the tape as projection begins.
5. Where any intermissions will occur.
6. Procedures for incidental music, light-show effects, and so on.
7. Any special projection effects needed, such as "Run titles at slow speed" or "Hold red filter in front of lens for the murder scene."
8. Warning if sound is stripped.

Typical entries on a cue sheet might be:

(6) *City Steel*, 12 minutes, 8mm, Tape 1, red leader, start at 424

(7) *Jogging*, 6 minutes, Super 8, Tape 2, green leader, start at 52

(8) *Car Crash*, 9 minutes, 16mm, sound striped

Each squad should have certain jobs to do that mesh with those of the other groups but not overlap.

The lighting group: In charge of house lights, which should be raised on cue at the end of each film and lowered only on a signal from the projection crew.

The projection group: Should have equipment set up with projectors focused and the first film ready to go well in advance of the audience's arrival. Equipment should include an extra take-up reel, a small flashlight, pincers (from drug store) to take out jammed film, an adapter for three-prong sockets, an extension cord, a rack for reels of film to be projected, an extra projection bulb, and a check list of major equipment required. Two dual-8 projectors plus a 16mm, if needed, will allow for the most flexibility in programming and give the best coverage in case of a projector breakdown. When a film is being shown on one projector, another should be threaded with the next film. Short films or excerpts can be spliced on a common reel to further expedite projection. Leader should be fed through until it reaches the point of projection before the projection light is turned on. The light should be turned off as soon as the film ends to avoid showing white leader on the screen. The films, numbered in sequence, should be kept in an easily accessible rack.

The sound group: Should have its recorder or recorders set up somewhere in the vicinity of the screen but where the operators can spot signals both from the projection group and from whoever is coordinating the program. 16mm speakers should be placed directly below the screen. Sound tests should be conducted before the audience arrives. As many sound tracks as possible should be spliced together in correct sequence on one or more master tapes, each track separated from the next by a length of colored leader tape.

There should be set procedures for each group to follow in the event of an equipment failure or if a splice breaks on either a film or tape.

Dead spots in the evening should be avoided. There might be a festival overture to precede the first half of the program and another after the intermission. These could be tapes created by the group enhanced by projected slides or light-show effects, or they could be music from the sound tracks of professional films. One film should follow the other in a businesslike manner, and speeches, remarks from the stage, and so on, should be cut to a minimum so that the cinema conventions the audience is used to are preserved as much as possible.

BIBLIOGRAPHY

I. Technical and Professional Books on Film Making

There are not many books that are directly of use to the teacher and student of film making in the schools. The first two books on this list have useful ideas, but little technical information on the Super 8 and 8mm film systems and their use in the early grades. The other books listed are more advanced technically than is necessary or generally desirable for children's films. Teachers and advanced students should, however, find them helpful.

Ferguson, Robert. *How to Make Movies — A Practical Guide to Group Film-Making.* New York: Viking Press, 1969.

Lowndes, Douglas. *Film Making in Schools.* London: B. T. Batsford (distributed in New York by Watson-Guptill), 1968.

American Society of Cinematographers. *American Cinematographer Manual.* 2nd ed. Hollywood: 1968.

Bomback, R.H., ed. *Handbook of Amateur Cinematography.* London: Fountain Press, 1958.

Brodbeck, Emil E. *Handbook of Basic Motion-picture Techniques.* Philadelphia: Chilton, 1966.

Grosset, Philip. *The Complete Book of Amateur Film Making.* London: Evans Bros. Ltd., 1967.

Kepes, Gyorgy, ed. *The Nature and Art of Motion.* New York: George Braziller, 1965. (Vision and Value series.)

Larson, Rodger, and Ellen Meade. *Young Filmmakers.* New York: E. P. Dutton, 1969.

Mascelli, Joseph V. *The Five C's of Cinematography.* Hollywood: Cine/Grafic Publications, 1966. (The C's are camera angles, continuity, cutting, close-ups, composition.)

Oringel, Robert S. *Audio Control Handbook.* New York: Hastings House, 1963.

Petzold, Paul. *All-in-One Cine Book.* London and New York: Focal Plane Press, 1969.

Trapnell, Coles. *Teleplay.* San Francisco: Chandler Publishing Co., 1966.

A group of texts published in London by Focal Press and distributed in New York by Hastings House includes the following:

Baddeley, W. Hugh. *The Technique of Documentary Film Production.* 1967.

Fielding, Raymond. *The Technique of Special Effects Cinematography.* 1967.

Hapas, John, and Roger Manvell. *The Technique of Film Animation.* 1968.

Huntley, John, and Roger Manvell. *The Technique of Film Music.* 1967.

Kehoe, Vincent J.-R. *The Technique of Film and Television Make-up.* 1967.

Nisbett, Alex. *The Technique of the Sound Studio.* 1967.

Reisz, Karel, and Gavin Millar. *The Technique of Film Editing.* 1968.

II. Manuals

This is a short list of the kind of movie-making manuals designed for the amateur that are generally available in camera shops. Some of them should be helpful for special problems in the film class.

Current, Ira B., F.P.S.A. *Electric Eye Movie Manual.* New York: Amphoto (distributed by Hastings House), 1961.

Duitz, Murray. *Better 8mm Home Movie Guide.* Philadelphia: Chilton, 1960.

Gaskill, Arthur L., and David A. Englander. *How to Shoot a Movie Story — The Technique of Pictorial Continuity.* New York: Morgan and Morgan, 1960.

Matzkin, Myron A. *Better Super 8 Movie Making.* New York: Amphoto (distributed by Hastings House), 1967.

Norinsky, Sid. *The Amateur's 8mm Movie Guide.* New York: Universal Photo Books, 1961.

A collection of books for the amateur film maker is the Fountain Moviebook series, published in London by Fountain Press. It includes such titles as *Choosing and Using a Cine Camera, How to Use 8mm,* and *Filming the Family.*

III. Filmography

A basic aid to teachers of the film is *A Filmography of Films about Movies and Moviemaking,* available from Dept. 1454, Eastman Kodak Company, 343 State Street, Rochester, N.Y. Listed are films on all aspects of moviemaking, from basic techniques to aesthetics, with information on the availability of each film.

IV. Reference Books

The following selection of books about films and film making as an art form should be helpful in establishing the core of a film library for a film club or classroom. They are concerned with the aesthetics and history of the "movies" and with outstanding film artists.

Battcock, Gregory, ed. *The New American Cinema — A Critical Anthology.* New York: E. P. Dutton, 1967.

Bazin, Andre. *What Is Cinema?* Berkeley: University of California Press, 1967.

Houston, Penelope. *The Contemporary Cinema.* Middlesex, England: Penguin Books, 1963.

Jacobs, Lewis. *The Rise of the American Film: A Critical History with an Essay on the Rise of the Experimental Cinema in America, 1921-1947.* New York: Teachers College Press, Columbia University, 1967.

Knight, Arthur. *The Liveliest Art — A Panoramic History of the Movies.* New York and Toronto: New American Library, Mentor Book, 1957.

Manvell, Roger. *New Cinema in the USA — The Feature Film since 1946.* New York: E. P. Dutton, 1968.

Montagu, Ivor. *Film World — A Guide to Cinema.* Baltimore: Penguin Books, 1964.

Renan, Sheldon. *An Introduction to the American Underground Film.* New York: E. P. Dutton, 1967.

Robinson, W. R., ed. *Man and the Movies.* Baton Rouge: Louisiana State University Press, 1967.

Sarris, Andrew. *The American Cinema: Directors and Directions, 1929-1968.* New York: E. P. Dutton, 1968.

Stearn, Gerald Emanuel, ed. *McLuhan: Hot & Cool, A Primer for the Understanding of & A Critical Symposium with a Rebuttal by McLuhan.* New York: New American Library, Signet Book, 1967.

Two groups of paperbacks concerned with film directors are the Movie Editions series, edited by Ian Cameron, published at Berkeley by the University of California Press, and the Cinema One series, published in conjunction with the British Film Institute in England by Secker & Warburg and distributed in New York by Doubleday. Movie Editions titles include: Raymond Durgnat, *Bunuel*; and Joel Finler, *Stroheim*. Cinema One titles include: Richard Roud, *Godard*; Tom Milne (ed.), *Losey on Losey*; and Geoffrey Nowell-Smith, *Visconti*.

V.   Periodicals

Listed are magazines concerned with all aspects of the film and film making.

Audiovisual Instruction. National Education Association, Dept. of Audio-visual Instruction, 1201 16th St., N.W., Washington, D.C.

Media and Methods. Media & Methods Institute, Inc., 134 N. 13th Street, Philadelphia, Pa.

Eight mm. Magazine. Haymarket Press, Gillon House, 9 Harrow Road, London, W. 2, England.

Film Comment. 838 West End Ave., New York City.

Film Culture. Jonas Mekas, Box 1499, G.P.O., New York City.

Film Library Quarterly. Film Library Information Council, 101 West Putnam Ave., Greenwich, Conn.

Film News. Film News Co., Editorial and Advertising Office, 259 W. 57th St., New York City.

Film Quarterly. University of California Press, Berkeley, Calif.

Film Society Review. 144 Bleecker St., New York City.

Films and Filming. Hansom Books, 16 Buckingham Palace Rd., London, S.W. 1, England.

Sight and Sound: The International Film Quarterly. British Film Institute, 81 Dean St., London, W. 1, England.

Sightlines. Educational Film Library Association, 17 West 60th St., New York City.

Three newsletters of interest to film makers are:
Making Films in New York. 120 E. 56th St., New York City.

New York Film Maker's Newsletter. Film Makers Distribution Center, 175 Lexington Ave., New York City.

Canyon Cinema News. 263 Colgate, Berkeley, Calif.

VI.   Film Organizations, Film Lists, Film Distributors

The following will help to extend the field of film making beyond the limitations of this book. Here can be found distributors of significant films, exhibition places, festival news, and general information about the current film world.

Organizations

American Federation of Film Societies, 144 Bleecker St., New York City.
Canadian Film Institute, 1762 Carling Ave., Ottawa 3, Ontario, Canada.
Children's Cultural Foundation, Inc., 325 E. 57th St., New York City.

Educational Film Library Association, 250 West 57th St., New York City.

The International Center of Films for Children, UNESCO, 24 Rue Royale, Brussels 3, Belgium.

National Center of Films for Children, 6066 Aspinwall Rd., Oakwood, Calif.

National Film Board of Canada, P.O. Box 6100, Montreal 3, Quebec, Canada.

The National Film Study Project, John M. Culkin, S.J., Director, Center for Communications, Fordham University, Bronx, New York.

National Screen Education Committee, 16 Trowbridge St., Cambridge, Mass.

New York State Council in the Arts, 250 West 57th St., New York City.

UNESCO, Place de Fontenay, Paris, France.

Selected Film Lists

Films for Libraries. American Librarian Association, Audio-Visual Board, Chicago, Illinois.

Films for Children. Educational Film Library Association, 250 West 57th St., New York City.

Films for Children: A Selected List and *Films for Young Adults: A Selected List.* New York Library Association, 20 West 53rd St., New York City.

Tell It Like It Is. Enoch Pratt Free Library, 400 Cathedral St., Baltimore, Md.

"Winning Teen Age Movies," *Library Journal,* Nov. 15, 1968, p. 4339.

Catalogues of Short Films and Filmstrips. Renan, UNESCO, Dept. of Mass Communications, No. 14, 1955, No. 44, 1963.

Films, a catalog of the film collection in the New York Public Library. The Film Library, Donnell Library Center, 20 West 53rd St., New York City.

Selected Film Distributors

ACI Films Inc., 16 W. 46th St., New York City.

Brandon Films, 221 W. 57th St., New York City.

Children's Cultural Foundation, 325 E. 57th St., New York City.

Cinema 16 Film Library, 80 University Place, New York City.

Contemporary Films Inc. (McGraw Hill), 267 W. 25th St., New York City.

Grove Press Film Division, 80 University Place, New York City.

The Janus Film Library, 24 W. 58th St., New York City.

Leacock, Pennebaker, Inc., 56 W. 45th St., New York City.

Museum of Modern Art Film Library, 11 West 53rd St., New York City.

Trans-world Films, 332 South Michigan Ave., Chicago, Illinois.

Yellow Ball Workshop, 62 Tarbell Ave., Lexington, Massachusetts.

INDEX